About this Learning Guide

CW01590488

Shmoop Will Make You a Better Lover*
*of Literature, History, Poetry, Life...

Our lively learning guides are written by experts and educators who want to show your brain a good time. Shmoop writers come primarily from Ph.D. programs at top universities, including Stanford, Harvard, and UC Berkeley.

Want more Shmoop? We cover literature, poetry, bestsellers, music, US history, civics, biographies (and the list keeps growing). Drop by our website to see the latest.

www.shmoop.com

Table of Contents

Introduction

In a Nutshell

When *To Kill a Mockingbird*'s story of an African-American man falsely accused of raping a white woman first appeared in 1960, the Civil Rights Movement was well on its way toward significantly revolutionizing how the U.S. conceived of race. In 1954, the Supreme Court ruled in *Brown vs. the Board of Education* that separate was not equal, paving the way for the integration of the public school system. In 1955, Rosa Parks refused to give up her seat on a bus to a white person and was arrested, sparking a series of boycotts that were ultimately successful in changing policy. Progress was far from smooth, however: in 1958 some southern schools closed altogether, rather than let African-Americans study alongside whites. And, in 1955, fourteen-year-old Emmett Till was brutally murdered after approaching a white woman in a store – an event that may have influenced author Harper Lee in writing *To Kill a Mockingbird*.

Lee did not set her novel in contemporary late 1950s society, however. This novel instead takes place a few decades earlier, before the changes and conflicts of the Civil Rights era. During this period, America was watching closely the infamous Scottsboro Trials, in which two impoverished white women accused nine young black men of rape. These trials may have been one of several influences on Lee as she crafted the *Mockingbird* story. The book is set in the time period of Lee's own youth, and many critics have pointed out the similarities between her and Scout, and her childhood friend, Truman Capote, and Dill. Lee herself has said that she did not intend the book to be an autobiography. She simply wrote what she knew. It's also her only book: she never published another novel, and, within a few years of *Mockingbird*'s publication, she went into a seclusion to rival that of her character Boo Radley. (For more on Lee's childhood, see Shmoop's Harper Lee Biography).

If a person's only going to write one novel, they couldn't do much better than *Mockingbird*. Awarded the Pulitzer Prize, it's also never been out of print, and has long been a staple of high school English classes. On at least one list of top-whatever books, it's ranked #1. The novel has become an iconic example of a book that can make its readers into better people in 300 pages or less.

While *Mockingbird*'s message of standing up for what's right even when the costs are high still receives acclaim, not everyone agrees that it holds the moral high ground. While the main reason it frequently appears on the ALA's list of banned books is its use of profanity, it's also been challenged for its one-dimensional representation of African-Americans as docile, simple folk who need whites to protect them. While some see the novel as a powerful statement against racism, others see it as reproducing racism in a less obvious form. No matter which side a reader leans towards, the strong reactions the novel provokes just go to show that its influence remains strong even today.

Why Should I Care?

One of the most infuriating things we hear as kids, usually from obnoxiously smug adults, is "Life isn't fair." The feeling behind this sentence usually isn't "but it should be, so let's get working on that," but rather "that's the way grown-ups roll – suck it up and deal, kid." And as we get older, we start believing that that's just the way it is, and nothing we can do will change it.

To Kill a Mockingbird portrays a society that is supremely, staggeringly unfair: the U.S. South in the 1930s in a small town where racism is part of the very fabric of society. Faced with this situation, an equality-minded person might be tempted to say, "Screw it, wake me up when the Civil Rights Movement gets here," and keep his or her head down until then.

Some people in the novel do just that. But a few decide to do what they can to take action on the side of justice and equality, even though they think it's mostly hopeless. *To Kill a Mockingbird* doesn't sugarcoat the results (minor spoiler: the book does not end with African-Americans and whites holding hands and singing "It's a Small World"). It does, however, suggest that doing something to make life a little more fair, even if it seems like it's not having any effect, is still worthwhile, and what's more, admirable.

Summary

Book Summary

The place: Maycomb, Alabama. As our narrator describes it, Maycomb could be a finalist for the Most Boring Town in America. Few people move in, fewer move out, so it's just the same families doing the same things for generation after generation. One such family is the Finches: Scout, her brother Jem, and their father Atticus. Every summer Scout and Jem are joined by Dill Harris, who shares their obsession with the local haunted house, the Radley Place, and the boogeyman who lives there, Boo Radley. Jem makes up hair-raising stories about Boo's bloodthirsty ways, but that just makes Dill want to see him all the more.

Fall comes, Dill leaves, and Scout starts school. The Radley Place is in between Scout's house and school, so she has to go by it every day, usually at top speed. One day she notices something odd: a couple of pieces of gum stuck in a hole in the tree. She tells Jem about it, and soon they find other treasures hidden in the same place, including finely-carved soap figurines of Scout and Jem themselves. This lasts until the following fall, when they find that Mr. Nathan (Boo's brother) has filled in the knothole with cement.

That winter, disaster strikes: Miss Maudie's house catches on fire and burns to the ground. While a sleepy Scout stands on the street trying not to freeze, someone drapes a blanket over her shoulders without her noticing: turns out that someone was Boo Radley, and it freaks Scout out that he was right there and she didn't even notice.

At school, Scout gets flak from her classmates because her father, a lawyer, has taken on a new client, an African-American man named Tom Robinson. Atticus tells her that a lot of people think he shouldn't defend Tom because of his race, but that it's the right thing to do. At his request, Scout stops fighting her classmates to defend her father's honor, even though they call her a coward.

Christmas comes, and Scout and Jem get their dream gifts: a pair of air rifles. Atticus won't teach them to shoot, but he tells them that if they must shoot at birds, they shouldn't pick on mockingbirds, which don't do anyone any harm. The kids feel kind of dissatisfied with boring old Dad, who can't do any of the cool things (like playing football or training ninjas) that the other fathers do. One day a mad dog turns up on their street, and Atticus reluctantly shoots it. The kids are surprised to learn that their father is a crack shot, since he's never told them anything about it.

One week Atticus is out of town for a Sunday, so the family's cook, Calpurnia, takes the kids to her own African-American church, First Purchase. Everyone welcomes them except a woman named Lula, who says that they don't belong there. The priest, Reverend Sykes, holds a collection to support Tom Robinson's family, and doesn't let anyone leave the church until he's sure they have enough money. Later Scout asks Calpurnia what Tom is accused of, and Cal reluctantly tells her that Bob Ewell has accused him of raping Ewell's daughter. The kids talk to Calpurnia about her past and realize that she has a whole other life that they don't know anything about.

When they get home from church, they find Aunt Alexandra, who's come to stay with them for a while. She has two goals: to teach the kids some family pride, and to get Scout to be a proper lady. Both goals seem doomed from the start.

One evening a week later, Mr. Tate and some other men turn up at the Finch house to talk to Atticus about the Robinson case. Their manner scares Jem and Scout, but Atticus assures them that the men are friendly. But the next evening Atticus goes out, and when the kids go looking for him they find him sitting in front of the jail where Tom is held. They're about to head home when some men pull up, who want Atticus to get out of the way so they can get to Tom. Atticus refuses to move, and Scout thinks something exciting is going to happen so she runs up to him, with Jem and Dill on her heels. It's only then she realizes this is a different group of men from the ones that turned up at her house, and they are definitely not friendly. But her innocent attempts at conversation deflect the men's anger, and they leave without violence.

The next day is Tom Robinson's trial. Atticus tells the kids to stay home, so they just sit on their porch and watch everyone go by on the way to the courthouse – apparently the trial is the must-see event of the season. After lunch the kids head over to the courthouse. They can't find a seat, so Reverend Sykes takes them to sit with him in the balcony segregated for African-Americans.

At the trial, Sheriff Tate testifies that Mr. Ewell and his daughter Mayella told him that Tom had beaten and raped Mayella, but that he hadn't called a doctor to examine her. Tate also says that Mayella's worst injuries were on the right side of her face. Then Mr. Ewell, who reminds Scout of a rooster, takes the stand and says basically the same thing, only with more offensive language. Atticus gets Ewell to write something, showing that he is left-handed.

Mayella is the next witness. She gives her version of the crime. Atticus's first questions to her are less about what happened than about her home life more generally, showing how lonely it is. Atticus has Tom stand up so Mayella can identify him, and Scout sees that Tom's left hand is shriveled and useless. Mayella breaks down under questioning and then refuses to answer Atticus's questions at all.

Finally Tom Robinson, the only witness for the defense, is up for questioning. Tom gives a very different version of events, in which Mayella was trying to kiss him despite his refusals when Mr. Ewell showed up and Tom ran. During Mr. Gilmer's cross-examination of Tom, Dill starts crying, and Jem makes Scout take him outside. There they run into Mr. Dolphus Raymond, whose sympathizes with Dill's sick anger at the condescending way Mr. Gilmer was treating Tom.

Dill and Scout return to the courtroom to find Atticus well into his closing remarks. Jem whispers that Atticus has just gone over the evidence and there's no way they can lose. Atticus tells the jury that the prosecution is relying on the jury's racism to convict Tom even though there's no evidence any crime even took place. Mayella's injuries at the time suggested that she was beaten by a left-handed man, and Tom's left hand is useless (though Mr. Ewell's isn't). Atticus reminds the jury that everyone should be equal under the law, and they should do their duty and acquit Tom. After four hours of deliberation, the jury finally delivers its verdict: guilty. As Atticus walks down the aisle and out of the courtroom, the African-Americans in the balcony silently stand up as a gesture of respect.

Atticus and Jem especially are bitterly disappointed at the verdict, but they feel a little better the next morning. At breakfast it turns out that a large segment of the local African-American population has sent gifts of food to the Finches. Not everyone is so grateful, though: when Atticus runs into Ewell in town that morning, Ewell spits in his face and tells him to watch out for worse.

Atticus isn't scared of Ewell, but the kids are terrified. Atticus calms them down, and tells them that Tom is at a prison 70 miles away, but he can appeal the ruling. Jem and Atticus talk about the legal system, and how it happened that the jury could convict Tom when he was so obviously innocent. Atticus also tells them that there was one man who wanted to acquit Tom – a friend of the Mr. Cunningham whom Scout talked to in the lynching party – but he couldn't hold out against everyone else.

At the end of August, Aunt Alexandra hosts a missionary tea, and Scout ends up joining the party. Two of the visitors, Mrs. Merriweather and Mrs. Farrow, talk about the Robinson case and in a polite, ladylike way accuse Atticus of stirring up trouble by defending Tom, before moving on to the general inferiority of black people. Miss Maudie cuts them down to size.

Atticus comes home early and calls Calpurnia and Aunt Alexandra aside. Scout and Miss Maudie follow them into the kitchen to hear that Tom is dead – shot while trying to climb over the prison fence right in front of the guards. Atticus takes Calpurnia to go tell Tom's wife Helen, and the other women grimly return to the tea party.

Later, Scout hears a rumor that Ewell said that Tom wasn't the only one who ought to be taken out and shot. In the meantime Ewell has also been keeping up his grudge campaign, harassing Helen Robinson (until Link Deas makes him stop) and possibly Judge Taylor.

One dark night Jem and Scout are on their way back home from the school's Halloween pageant when they hear someone following them. Suddenly they're attacked, though Scout can't see much because of her costume. When things calm down, one man is on the ground, and another carries the injured and unconscious Jem back to the Finch house, while Scout follows.

At home Aunt Alexandra calls the doctor and Atticus calls the sheriff. Dr. Reynolds arrives and treats Jem; then Mr. Tate comes in and tells them that he's found the corpse of Mr. Ewell at the site of the attack. Scout tells them what she heard, and realizes that the fourth man – still standing in the room – is Boo Radley.

Atticus thinks that Jem killed Ewell and starts planning his legal defense. Tate says it wasn't Jem, but Atticus says he won't let Tate hush it up. Tate eventually convinces Atticus that Jem wasn't the one who did it, and it would be a sin to drag Boo through a court case. Atticus finally gives in, though he's worried Scout won't understand why.

Scout walks Boo home at his request, and then looks at her neighborhood with new eyes from the Radley front porch, thinking about how recent events would have appeared to Boo from this vantage point.

Scout returns home and snuggles up with Atticus, who reads aloud to her until she falls asleep.

Chapter One

- The story begins with an injury: the narrator's brother Jem got his arm broken when he was thirteen.
- While the arm is never quite as good as new, it doesn't interfere with Jem's mad football skills, so he doesn't care much.
- Years afterward, brother and narrator argue over where the story really starts: the narrator blames it on the Ewell family, while Jem (the older sibling by four years) puts the beginning at the summer they first met Dill.
- The flash-forward conversation continues: the narrator says that if you want to get technical about it, everything began with Andrew Jackson, whose actions led to their forefather Simon Finch settling where they did.
- The flash-forward becomes a flashback: Simon Finch was a pious and miserly Englishman who left his home country to wander around America, before settling in Alabama with his accumulated wealth, his family, and his slaves.
- Simon's homestead was called Finch's Landing, and was a mostly self-sufficient estate run by Simon's male descendents, selling cotton to buy what the farm couldn't produce itself.
- The wealth went away with the Civil War, but the tradition of living off the land at Finch's Landing remained.

- The current generation, however, has bucked the trend: Atticus, the narrator's father, studied law in Montgomery, while his younger brother went all the way to Boston to become a doctor.
- The only Finch left at the Landing is their sister Alexandra and her quiet, inactive husband.
- After becoming a lawyer, Atticus returned to Maycomb, the county seat of Maycomb County, twenty miles from Finch's landing.
- Atticus saved his money to put his younger brother through med school.
- Atticus feels at home in Maycomb, not least because he's related to nearly everyone in the town.
- Out of the flashback, into the present-time of the story (which we already know the narrator's actually remembering: hop over to "Point of View/Narrative Voice" if you want the 411 on that right now).
- The narrator thinks about the Maycomb s/he (we don't know which yet) knew: it's not a happening place. Everyone moves slower than sweat, and there's not much worth hurrying for, let alone much sense of what might be happening outside the county lines.
- The narrator lives on the town's main residential drag with her brother Jem, her father Atticus, and their cook Calpurnia, who is a force to be reckoned with.
- You may notice there's no mom to be found: she died when the narrator was two, and the narrator doesn't really remember her, though Jem does.
- The story really gets underway the summer when the narrator is five going on six and Jem is nine going on ten.
- This is the summer Dill arrives in Maycomb.
- Their first meeting happens like this: Jem and the narrator are playing in their backyard, hear a noise next door, and go to check it out. The find a small boy, six going on seven but looking younger, who introduces himself as Charles Baker Harris and announces that he can read.
- Charles Baker Harris says that people call him Dill, so we will too.
- Dill tells the narrator and Jem a bit about himself: he's from Meridian, Mississippi, but he's spending the summer with his aunt, the young Finches' next-door neighbor Miss Rachel.
- Unlike the rural Finches, he's had access to movie theatres, and so he regales them with the story of Dracula.
- The narrator asks Dill about his father, who isn't dead but also isn't around. Dill gets a bit embarrassed about the dad question, so Jem tells his sibling to shut up.
- Dill, Jem, and the narrator spend the summer acting out stories from the books they've read, over and over and over, until they start to get bored.
- Dill comes to the rescue with a new idea: they can try to make Boo Radley come out.
- The Radley Place is the haunted house of the neighborhood, complete with ghost: Boo Radley, who got in trouble with the law as a teenager and has been holed up in the house unseen ever since. The kids think his family might be keeping him prisoner.
- The house has quite the reputation with the neighborhood kids, who avoid it at all costs.
- The narrator tells us a story about Boo that Jem got from Miss Stephanie Crawford, the neighborhood busybody: that Boo, then 33 years old, had been cutting out newspaper articles for his scrapbook when suddenly he stabbed the scissors into his father's leg, then calmly went back to what he was doing.
- After that Boo was locked up by the police briefly, and there was talk of sending him to an insane asylum, but he ended up back in the Radley Place.
- Still after that, old Mr. Radley, Boo's father, died, but he was soon replaced by Boo's

older brother Nathan, and nothing much changed at the Radley Place.
- Rumor has it that Boo gets out at night and stalks around the neighborhood, but none of the kids has ever actually seen him.
- Jem makes up horror stories about what Boo's like (think a cross between a vampire and a zombie), but Dill still wants to see him.
- Dill dares Jem to go knock on the Radleys' door.
- Jem tries to get out of it without showing he's scared, but gives in when Dill says he doesn't have to knock, just touch the door.
- Jem works up his nerve, dashes up to the house, slaps the door, and runs back at top speed without looking behind him.
- The three children, after getting to safety on their own porch, look at the Radley Place, but all they see is the hint of an inside shutter moving.

Chapter Two

- The summer ends and Dill heads back home to Meridian.
- The narrator looks forward to joining the kids at school for the first time instead of spying on them through a telescope like a pint-size stalker.
- Jem takes the narrator to school, and explains that it's different from home – and he doesn't want his first-grade sibling cramping his fifth-grade style.
- The narrator's teacher is a young woman by the name of Miss Caroline Fisher, who's from North Alabama, otherwise known to the native Maycombians as Crazy Land.
- Miss Caroline reads the class a story about cats, and seems blithely unaware that she's already completely lost her audience, a bunch of farm kids whom the narrator says are "immune to imaginative literature" (2.8).
- Miss Caroline puts the alphabet up on the board, which all of the class already knows (most of them are starting first grade for the second time).
- Miss Caroline asks the narrator to read, and is not pleased that she's already good at it.
- Miss Caroline assumes, despite the narrator's disagreement, that Atticus has taught the narrator how to read, and decrees that these lessons must stop because Atticus isn't a licensed teacher and therefore is doing his child more harm than good.
- The narrator gets the impression that reading, which seems to come as naturally as breathing, is something like a sin when it's done out of class.
- Trying to stay out of further trouble, the narrator zones out till recess, then complains to Jem.
- Jem says that Miss Caroline is at the center of educational reform in the school, which he calls "the Dewey Decimal System" (2.25).
- This new system results in boring class time, so the narrator starts writing (in cursive) a letter to Dill. Miss Caroline makes the narrator stop, saying that first graders print, and cursive isn't taught until third grade.
- The narrator remembers that Calpurnia had passed rainy days by giving writing lessons.
- Miss Caroline is halted in her inspection of her students' lunches by Walter Cunningham, who doesn't have one.
- She tries to lend him a quarter for lunch, but he refuses to take it.

- The narrator, whose name we now learn is Jean Louise, steps in, explaining to Miss Caroline that Walter is a Cunningham.
- That explanation, crystal clear to Jean Louise, doesn't mean much to Miss Caroline, so she explains further: the Cunninghams won't take anything from anybody, preferring to get by on the little they have.
- Flashback: Jean Louise knows about the Cunninghams because Walter's father hired Atticus to sort out an entailment on his property, and paid for the service by barter rather than in cash.
- Back to the schoolroom present: Jean Louise wants to explain everything properly, but doesn't have the ability, so she just says that Miss Caroline is making Walter ashamed by trying to lend him money he can't pay back.
- Miss Caroline cracks at this, and calls Jean Louise up to the front of the class, where she pats her hand with the ruler and makes her stand in the corner.
- The class breaks out laughing when they realize that the ruler taps were supposed to be corporal punishment.
- The bell rings and everyone leaves for lunch, with Miss Caroline collapsing with her head in her hands at her desk.

Chapter Three

- Jean Louise catches Walter Cunningham in the schoolyard and beats him up for being the reason she got in trouble, but Jem stops her.
- She explains to Jem (who calls her Scout, so we will too) what happened.
- Jem invites Walter to come home for lunch with Scout and him.
- At the Finch house, Atticus talks to Walter about farming problems on equal footing, while Jem and Scout listen half-comprehendingly.
- Walter asks for molasses, which he proceeds to pour all over his food.
- Scout asks him what the heck he's doing, and he stops in embarrassment.
- Calpurnia calls Scout into the kitchen, where she gives her a lecture on hospitality – Walter's a guest and so he can do whatever he wants without Scout judging him for having different manners from what she's used to.
- The kids go back to school, and Scout whiles away the afternoon by hating Calpurnia for having chewed her out.
- She's called back to the here and now by a shriek from Miss Caroline, who's seen a "cootie" (3.37) – probably a louse, which may sound more familiar in the plural, lice – on one of the students.
- Miss Caroline tries to send the student, named Burris Ewell, home to wash his hair (after looking up lice remedies in a reference book), and says he should take a bath (which he really needs, since he looks worse than Pigpen from Peanuts) before coming back to class the following day.
- Burris tells her that he's not coming back.
- Another student explains to the puzzled Miss Caroline that Burris is one of the Ewells, who come the first day to satisfy the truant officer but disappear from school after that.
- Burris decides he's already done with school for the year even though the first day isn't

over yet, and manages to make Miss Caroline cry before he leaves.

- The other students try to cheer Miss Caroline up, and she reads them another boring story.
- Scout, highly dissatisfied with her first day of school, goes home and makes plans to run away.
- Atticus comes home from work, having apparently forgotten about Scout's lunchtime misbehavior, and Calpurnia gets back on Scout's good side with tasty crackling bread.
- After dinner, Atticus invites Scout to come read with him, which reminds her of her run-in over reading with Miss Caroline that morning.
- Scout tries to convince Atticus that she doesn't really need to go to school, but he's not buying it.
- She tells him about her first day of school, and Atticus tells her to try to think about things from the other person's perspective – in this case, Miss Caroline, who was only trying to do her best in a strange place, whose ways she doesn't yet understand.
- Scout says that Burris Ewell stays home from school so she should be able to do so too, but Atticus says that what holds true for Ewells doesn't apply to Finches.
- Scout finally is appeased when Atticus proposes a compromise: they'll keep reading at home if she'll keep going to school – but she shouldn't tell Miss Caroline about it.

Chapter Four

- Scout thinks about all the people around her who seem to be doing just fine without having been taught through her school's reformed educational techniques.
- Every day Scout runs by the Radley Place to get home after school.
- One day she notices something, and works up the nerve to go back and look at it.
- A tree at the edge of the Radley yard has some tinfoil stuck to a knothole, and inside the hole Scout finds two pieces of chewing gum.
- She takes it home, and, after some testing to try to make sure it's not poisoned, she chews it, and does not immediately keel over and die.
- When Jem comes home (he doesn't get out of school till half an hour after Scout), he tells her to spit it out; when he finds out where she got the gum, he makes her gargle too.
- Finally, the last day of school comes, and the Finch kids look forward to the summer and the return of Dill.
- On their way home, they find another piece of tinfoil in the same knothole, and behind it a jewelry box, decorated with more tinfoil, containing two Indian-head pennies.
- Jem and Scout discuss the ethics of keeping their find: chewing gum is one thing, but money is something else entirely in their code of conduct.
- Soon Dill arrives, full of stories of his journey that may or may not be true – including news of his father.
- They talk about starting to play-act something, but already they're bored of everything they know.
- Dill says he can smell death, and tells Scout that her end is nigh.
- She tells him to shut up, and Jem mocks both of them for being (or pretending to be) superstitious.
- He talks about Hot Steams, who are ghosts who wander the earth because they can't get

to heaven, but Scout tells Dill not to believe him, which makes Jem mad.
- Scout suggests they play with a tire – sitting inside and being rolled around.
- Scout goes first, not realizing Jem's still angry at her, and he sends the tire-cramped Scout flying down the sidewalk.
- The tire bumps to a stop, and a dazed Scout extricates herself, only to realize that she's in the Radleys' front yard.
- As soon as she's able to find her feet she runs back to the boys, leaving Jem to pass the Radley gate once more to retrieve the tire she left behind.
- Calpurnia brings the kids lemonade, and Jem comes up with a new game: acting out the life and times of Boo Radley.
- The game starts out simple, but gets more and more complex as the summer goes on.
- One day Atticus walks up as they're performing the scissor-stabbing scene, and seems suspicious of their behavior, but doesn't explicitly forbid them from doing it.
- Scout still has qualms about going on with the game, especially since she's pretty sure that when she got dumped out of the tire she heard someone laughing inside the Radley house.

Chapter Five

- Scout convinces Jem to back off on the Radley game.
- Dill asks Scout to marry him, but then spends all his time hanging out with Jem, even though Scout tries to get his attention by beating him up, twice.
- Neglected by the boys, Scout spends her time hanging out with Miss Maudie Atkinson.
- Miss Maudie has a "tacit treaty" with the kids that she won't bother them if they don't bother her, so Scout's spending time with her is a first.
- A devoted gardener, Miss Maudie cultivates her yard with a passion.
- Miss Maudie makes the best cakes in the neighborhood, and best of all, shares them with the three kids.
- Scout asks Miss Maudie if she thinks Boo Radley is still alive, and Miss Maudie says she hasn't seen his coffin carried out yet, so he probably is.
- Flashback: Scout's Uncle Jack has a history of flirting with Miss Maudie, though in a joking way.
- Back to the present: Miss Maudie tells Scout more about the Radleys, including that old Mr. Radley (Boo's father) was a "foot-washing Baptist" (5.27), which is apparently much more hardcore than just regular Baptists.
- In fact, some of Mr. Radley's fellow foot-washers have told Miss Maudie that she and her flowers are going to burn in hell, because any time spent not reading the Bible is time spent in sin, especially if it involves creating something pleasing to the senses. (No word on whether criticizing one's neighbor's counts as a sin with them.)
- Miss Maudie says that the Radleys are "so busy worrying about the next world they've never learned to live in this one" (5.44), which accounts for some of their strangeness.
- Scout asks if Boo is crazy, and Miss Maudie says that if he wasn't when this whole thing started, he probably is now after being locked up for so long.
- Miss Maudie sends Scout home with some poundcake.

- Scout finally breaks into Jem and Dill's boys-only club, and finds out what they've been planning to do: try to put a note to Boo through one of the upper windows of the Radley Place using a fishing pole.
- Dill's going to be lookout with a bell to ring if anyone comes.
- Scout and Dill get into an argument as to whether all the stories Dill has told about his father are true.
- They put the plan into action, but Jem has some difficulty maneuvering the fishing pole, which is too short to reach the window.
- Scout hears Dill ringing the bell and turns around, expecting to see a slavering Boo Radley; instead, she sees Atticus, who is not pleased.
- Atticus tells the kids to stop bothering Boo, who has a perfect right to stay in his house if he wants to.
- Atticus also tells them to stop playing their stupid game, and Jem says they weren't making fun of Boo, inadvertently revealing to Atticus that they were in fact playing at being the Radleys.
- Jem eventually realizes he's been done in by the oldest lawyer's trick in the book.

Chapter Six

- Jem and Scout get permission from their father to go hang out with Dill at his aunt's fish pond, since Dill's leaving the next day.
- Scout suggests they watch for Mr. Avery, a neighbor who had previously astonished them by peeing in an impressive arc off his front porch.
- Dill suggests they go for a walk instead, and Scout, knowing that no one in Maycomb just goes for a walk, smells a rat.
- Jem says they're just going to go to the streetlight by the Radley Place.
- Once they get there Dill and Jem say they just want to peek in the window.
- Scout doesn't like this at all, but stops complaining when they accuse her of being a girl about it.
- The trio go under the wire fence at the back of the Radley Place and, after dealing with swishy collard greens, a squeaky gate, and clucking chickens, make it up to the house.
- Jem and Scout raise Dill up so he can look through the window, but he can't see much except curtains.
- Jem makes it onto the porch and looks through another window, when Scout sees a shadow – a man's shadow, moving across the porch towards Jem.
- The shadow goes up to Jem, raises his arm, drops it again, and then leaves.
- The kids, throwing caution to the winds, dash back the way they came.
- Scout trips as she hears a loud noise – someone's shooting at them.
- They dive under the fence, Jem leaving his pants behind when they get stuck on the wire.
- The kids make it home and see a bunch of neighbors gathered in front of the Radley Place.
- Realizing their absence will be noticed, they join the group.
- Miss Maudie tells them that Mr. Radley has been shooting at a "Negro" (6.60) in his yard.
- Suddenly everyone notices that Jem doesn't have any pants on.

- Dill tries to save the day by saying they were playing strip poker.
- Playing with cards apparently being more of a sin in Maycomb than stripping, Jem says that they were playing with matches.
- Atticus tells Jem to get his pants back, and Dill goes home, bidding his friends farewell.
- Scout goes to bed, but is terrified that every sound she hears might be Boo Radley coming to wreak his revenge.
- Jem gets up, telling Scout he's going back to get his pants.
- Scout threatens to wake Atticus, arguing that a beating isn't as bad as getting shot, but Jem refuses to back down.
- Scout sits outside on the porch, listening for the dreaded shotgun blast and waiting for Jem to return.
- Finally Jem returns – with his pants – and the two go back to bed.

Chapter Seven

- After his adventures at the Radley Place, Jem is in a bad mood for a week, and Scout doesn't get it, but leaves him alone.
- Scout starts second grade, whose only improvement over first grade is that she now gets out of school at the same time as Jem.
- Jem finally breaks his silence and tells Scout what happened when he went back to the Radley House: his pants weren't where he had left them, but were folded up on top of the fence, and the tear in them had been sloppily mended. Jem is thoroughly creeped out by this.
- Passing by the knothole tree, they see a ball of twine resting inside it.
- Scout wants to take it, but Jem thinks it might be someone's hiding spot and they should leave it alone.
- When the twine is still there after a few days, Jem takes it, and from then on there are no more qualms about taking things found in the knothole.
- A few months later, the knothole holds their best find yet: two figures carved out of soap that bear a striking resemblance to Scout and Jem.
- Scout throws them on the ground, thinking about voodoo dolls, but Jem rescues them.
- They try to figure out who might have made them, but can't think of anyone with both the skill and the desire to do so.
- The knothole haul in the following weeks just keeps getting better and better: a whole pack of chewing gum, a spelling bee medal, and a broken pocket watch (which Jem tries but fails to fix).
- Scout and Jem decide to write a letter to their secret benefactor.
- The next day, however, they find that the knothole has been filled with cement.
- Jem stakes out Mr. Nathan and finally catches him to ask if he was the cement-pourer.
- Mr. Nathan says that the tree's sick and the cement is an attempt to cure it.
- Later Jem asks Atticus about the tree, and Atticus says it looks healthy to him, but Mr. Radley should know his own trees.
- Jem stands on the porch till it gets dark, and Scout stays with him.
- When they finally go inside, Scout thinks Jem looks like he'd been crying, though she

hadn't heard a thing.

Chapter Eight

- Maycomb gets a season it hadn't seen in a while: winter.
- Mr. Avery tells the kids that bad children makes the seasons change, causing them to feel guilty.
- Mrs. Radley dies, but no one really notices, since they hardly saw her even when she was alive.
- Atticus goes to pay his condolences at the Radleys, and when he comes back Jem and Scout pounce on him to ask if he saw Boo in the flesh (he didn't).
- Scout is terrified when she wakes up one morning and sees white stuff pouring from the sky. Turns out it's snowing.
- School is cancelled, so Jem and Scout set out to make a snowman, though they don't really know how and there isn't much snow.
- The kids head over to Miss Maudie's to take her snow, running into Mr. Avery on the way, who reminds them that their sins are responsible for the unusual weather.
- Jem has a plan to make do with the minimal snowfall: he makes the snowman's guts out of mud, then coats the outside in a skin of snow so it looks like a real snowman.
- They add enough accessories to make their snowman instantly recognizable as a caricature of Mr. Avery, until Atticus makes them change it.
- That night, it's freezing.
- Atticus wakes Scout in the middle of the night because Miss Maudie's house – next door to the Finches' – is on fire.
- Atticus says they don't need to start taking their furniture out of the house yet, and that Jem should take Scout and go stand in front of the Radley Place, safe from the flames.
- Scout watches the men of the town trying to fight the fire and save some of Miss Maudie's belongings (Atticus carries out her most prized possession, a rocking chair), but it's a lost cause.
- Jem and Scout endure the intense cold and keep a close eye on Atticus: as long as he's not worried, they don't need to be either.
- Once the fire is finally put out (and Miss Maudie's house reduced to a smoking hole in the ground), the Finches return to their fortunately undamaged home.
- Atticus notices what Scout has so far failed to – that she's wrapped in a blanket that she didn't have when she left the house.
- Scout says that she stayed right where he told her to, in front of the Radley Place, but she and Jem saw Mr. Nathan fighting the fire, so if he wasn't the stealthy blanket-deliverer, it must have been some other occupant of that house. Hmm, who could that be?
- Jem tells Atticus all about the knothole and the cement and his mended pants.
- Atticus finally says outright that it must have been Boo Radley who brought the blanket, and Scout, who's been late for the clue train, is hit by belated terror to know that he was so close to her but she didn't even realize it.
- The next day, Jem and Scout stay home from school, and see Miss Maudie in her charred backyard.

- Miss Maudie, however, is a glass-half-full kind of person, and tells them that now she can rebuild her house the way she wants it. She's more worried about the trouble she's caused to neighborhood, and plans to smooth everything over with cake – except Miss Stephanie, who's putting her up till she gets her own place, can't have the recipe.

Chapter Nine

- Scout is ready to fight Cecil Jacobs on the schoolyard when he says that her father defends "niggers" (9.3). (This is the word the book uses, so we'll use it here, despite its history of offensiveness. See the "Speech and Dialogue" section in "Tools of Characterization" for a fuller explanation of how this term functions in the book.)
- Scout asks Jem about it, who tells her to ask Atticus.
- Later Scout does so, and Atticus tells her not to say "nigger."
- Scout then asks him if all lawyers defend Negroes, and he says that of course they do.
- Next Scout asks why if all lawyers do it Cecil made it sound worse than bootlegging (booze, not music), and Atticus explains the case.
- Atticus's client is a man named Tom Robinson, and he tries to explain to Scout the complexities of race relations in Maycomb.
- Atticus says that some people think he shouldn't be working hard at defending Tom Robinson, but for him it basically boils down to self-respect: he couldn't hold his head up if he caved to public opinion and did less than his best in the man's defense.
- Atticus asks Scout not to get in fights at school over the case, no matter what anyone says to her.
- Scout asks if they're going to win the case, and Atticus says no, but they have to try anyway.
- Atticus reassures Scout: "But remember this, no matter how bitter things get, they're [the residents of Maycomb are] still our friends and this is still our home" (9.27).
- The next day at school, Scout is about to fight Cecil Jacobs, but remembers what Atticus told her and walks away instead, even though she gets called a coward.
- Soon it's Christmas, which means a visit from Uncle Jack (good), but also a visit to Aunt Alexandra (bad).
- Even worse, it means having to spend time with Aunt Alexandra's grandson Francis, who is the yin to Scout's yang.
- Uncle Jack arrives with two long packages of mysterious contents.
- Scout cusses while Uncle Jack's around, and later he tells her that she shouldn't do that if she wants to grow up to be a lady (which she doesn't).
- The next day is Christmas morning, and they open the mysterious packages to find a pair of long-desired air rifles. (All together now: you'll shoot your eye out! Thanks, *A Christmas Story.*)
- Uncle Jack tells Atticus that he (Atticus) will have to teach them how to shoot, but Atticus says that that's his (Uncle Jack's) job.
- They head down to Finch's Landing, sans air rifles (to Scout's dismay, as she'd already had fantasies about shooting Francis).
- Old Simon Finch had given Finch Landing an interesting layout: the only way to get to his

daughters' room is by a staircase that leads into their parents' bedroom, meaning no sneaking out at night for the girls.

- Jem abandons his sister to schmooze with the adults, leaving Scout to deal with the dreaded Francis.
- They talk about their Christmas presents, and Francis is happy with his, though they are pretty much the boringest gifts you can think of.
- Scout thinks about Aunt Alexandra, who has strong ideas as to what girls should be that are very different from what Scout is (girls should wear frilly dresses instead of overalls, for example).
- It's dinnertime, and Scout alone is relegated to the kid's table.
- Despite the seating arrangement, Scout is happy to chow down on Aunt Alexandra's good eats.
- When all the adults (and Jem) are well into their food coma, Scout heads out to the backyard, joined by Francis.
- Scout brings up Dill, and defends him when Francis parrots his elders in putting him down.
- Francis then quotes Aunt Alexandra in calling Atticus a "nigger-lover" who's "ruinin' the family" (9.98).
- Scout holds her peace, lulling Francis into carelessness, and then pounces, beating him up good.
- Uncle Jack pulls Scout off Francis, and tells her she's in trouble, though he seems to care less about her punching her cousin than her swearing while she's doing it (as Francis helpfully tells their uncle, she called him a "whore-lady" [9.125]).
- Scout, Jem, Atticus, and Uncle Jack return to Maycomb, and Scout retreats to her room alone.
- Uncle Jack comes in to talk to Scout, who tells him he wasn't fair – he should have listened to both sides of the story, like Atticus always does, before passing judgment.
- Uncle Jack asks Scout to explain her side of the story, and she tells him what Francis had said to set her off.
- Uncle Jack wants to head right back to Finch's Landing to tell off Francis, but Scout stops him, saying that she doesn't want Atticus to know that she was fighting over someone insulting him after he told her not to.
- Scout asks Uncle Jack (who's a doctor) to bandage her still-bleeding hand.
- While he's doing that she asks him what a whore-lady is, but his answer doesn't tell her much.
- Later Scout overhears Uncle Jack and Atticus talking about her conversation with her uncle.
- Scout waits for Uncle Jack to break his promise and tell Atticus why she was fighting, but he doesn't.
- Atticus tells Uncle Jack some things about children: you should answer them truthfully and simply when they ask you questions, and bad language is less dangerous than hotheadedness.
- Atticus says that Scout needs to learn to control her temper because things are only going to get harder, but at least she's trying, and she does all right when she follows Jem's example.
- Uncle Jack asks Atticus how bad things are going to get, and Atticus tells him "it couldn't be worse" (9.182) – the whole case is based on he-said-she-said.
- Atticus says that he's just going to try to get the jury to think a little, and then have a better

chance to win the case on appeal.
- He also says that he'd rather not have taken the case, but once it was offered to him he couldn't refuse it in good conscience.
- Atticus hopes he can get his kids through the case without their "catching Maycomb's usual disease" – going "stark raving mad when anything involving a Negro comes up" (9.187) – and that they will come to him if they have questions.
- Atticus then tells Scout, still lurking around the corner eavesdropping, to go to bed, and many years later an older Scout realizes that her father meant her to overhear the conversation.

Chapter Ten

- Jem and Scout think their father is really old and can't do anything interesting, or even play football, like the other kids' fathers do.
- Even though he's really boring (they think), he still manages to give them trouble through his insistence on defending Tom Robinson, which their peers are gossiping about.
- It doesn't help that word has gotten around after Scout walked away from Cecil Jacobs that she wouldn't fight anymore, though she makes an exception for family members like Francis Hancock – they're fair game.
- Atticus refuses to teach Scout and Jem how to shoot their shiny new air rifles, so Uncle Jack gives them a shooting lesson.
- Atticus tells Jem that if he must shoot at birds, he should aim for the bluejays, but "it's a sin to kill a mockingbird" (10.7).
- Scout talks to Miss Maudie about how their neighborhood is all old people, and Miss Maudie (while bristling at being called old), acknowledges that there aren't any 20- or 30-somethings around to give Scout role models of young adulthood.
- Scout complains that Atticus can't do much of everything, and Miss Maudie tries to defend Atticus (he's a checkers grand master! he can play the Jew's Harp!), but Scout is not impressed.
- Scout goes home and builds a barricade from which to aim at Miss Maudie's butt across the street; Atticus finds her, and gets that it's a joke, but tells her not to aim at people anyway.
- Scout asks Calpurnia about her father's talents, and the cook is convinced that he has them, but draws a blank when asked to provide specifics.
- Jem is depressed when his father refuses to join in on the town's Methodists vs. Baptists football game and he has to stand on the sideline watching Cecil Jacobs's father making touchdowns for the opposing side (the Baptists).
- One day Jem and Scout go off exploring to see if they find any of the local wildlife to kill with their air rifles when they see Tim Johnson, a dog who belongs to Mr. Harry Johnson.
- The dog's acting kind of strange, so they run home to tell Calpurnia.
- Calpurnia at first tells them to deal with it themselves, but when she sees the dog for herself she dashes for the phone to tell Atticus that there's a mad dog on the loose.
- Then she talks to Miss Eula May, the town telephone operator, to tell her to let everyone else on the street know that they should stay out of the way of the rabid animal.

- The Radleys don't have a phone, so Calpurnia runs over to their place, bangs on their front door, and when no one answers, shouts, "Mad dog's comin'!" (10.72).
- As Calpurnia sprints back to the Finch house, Atticus and Mr. Heck Tate, the sheriff, arrive.
- The street is eerily quiet and empty, as its residents watch the dog's approach silently from their windows.
- The dog finally gets within range of Heck Tate's rifle, but he wants Atticus to make the shot, because if he misses the bullet will hit the Radley Place, and Mr. Tate knows he can't shoot that well.
- Atticus says he hasn't shot a gun in thirty years, but reluctantly takes the weapon when Mr. Tate thrusts it on him.
- Jem and Scout watch as their father walks out to the middle of the street, takes aim, fires, and kills the dog.
- The neighborhood residents slowly emerge from their houses now that the danger has passed, and Miss Maudie calls Atticus "One-Shot Finch" (10.122).
- Jem is shocked at his father's display of skill.
- Miss Maudie tells Jem and Scout that far from being the helpless old man they thought he was, Atticus "was the deadest shot in Maycomb County in his time" and his nickname was "Ol' One-Shot" (10.137).
- Scout and Jem wonder why they've never heard their father talk about his shooting skill, let alone actually use it.
- Miss Maudie tells them that Atticus feels that his marksmanship is a God-given talent that gives him an unfair advantage over other living creatures, and that he shouldn't use it unless he has to.
- The dog's body is taken away by a man named Zeebo.
- Scout wants to brag to everyone at school about her father's shooting skill, but Jem tells her not to, because he thinks Atticus wouldn't want her to, since he's never mentioned it before.
- Jem says that he wouldn't care if Atticus couldn't do anything, because, as he says, "Atticus is a gentleman, just like me!" (10.152).

Chapter Eleven

- Now that Scout's a grown-up second-grader, tormenting Boo Radley seems like little kid stuff, and she's setting her sights beyond the neighborhood to the metropolis of downtown Maycomb.
- Getting downtown, however, requires getting past the house of Mrs. Henry Lafayette Dubose, which is no walk in the park.
- Jem and Scout both hate the old woman, who hurls insults at them every time they pass her house, no matter how nice they are to her.
- Since Jem has made it a point of pride to get past Mrs. Dubose on the way to meeting Atticus when he gets off of work in the evenings, Atticus often finds them upset at her rantings.
- Atticus always stops and makes polite conversation with Mrs. Dubose, which makes Scout think he's incredibly brave.

- The day after Jem turns twelve he's got a load of birthday cash to spend, so they head down to town for him to lighten his pockets.
- On the list of purchases: a toy steam engine for Jem and a baton for Scout.
- As they pass Mrs. Dubose, she accuses them of playing hooky, even though it's Saturday.
- Jem and Scout hold firm while Mrs. Dubose abuses them, but when she attacks their father for defending Tom Robinson, Jem almost loses it and has to be dragged away by Scout.
- They make their purchases and head home, passing by Mrs. Dubose's house again.
- She's not on the front porch, and Jem suddenly snaps, grabs Scout's new baton, and uses it to destroy Mrs. Dubose's camellias, finally breaking the baton over his knee.
- They don't go to meet their father that evening, and Scout tries to cheer Jem up, but it's no use.
- Atticus comes home and asks Jem about what he did.
- He tells his son that no matter what she said, wreaking havoc upon an old lady's garden is not justifiable, and he should go over and talk to her – right now.
- Atticus stops Scout from joining her brother, so she sits there wondering why Atticus doesn't seem as worried as she is that the gun-toting Mrs. Dubose will make Jem pay for her camellias in blood.
- Scout finally climbs up on her father's lap and speaks her mind, and her father says that it's not fair, but they need to keep their heads, for things are only going to get worse as the Tom Robinson case gets closer.
- Atticus tells Scout that he hopes that when they're older they'll understand better why he's doing what he's doing.
- Scout tells Atticus he must be wrong, because most of the townspeople think he is.
- Atticus says that they're entitled to their opinions, but personal conscience isn't a democracy.
- Jem returns, saying that he cleaned up Mrs. Dubose's yard and apologized, even though he didn't mean it.
- Atticus says that there's no point in apologizing unless it's sincere, and that as a sick old lady Mrs. Dubose can't be held responsible for her actions.
- Jem says that Mrs. Dubose wants him to come over every day except Sunday to read to her, and Atticus says he has to do it.
- Jem says that "it's all dark and creepy" (11.67) inside the house, and Atticus says he should just pretend he's in the Radley Place.
- On Monday Jem heads over to Mrs. Dubose's house for his first round of reading, and Scout goes with him.
- They find her in bed, and she gets in a few sharp words before Jem starts reading.
- Scout finds her face disgusting – wrinkled, spotty, toothless, and drooling – and tries to find something else to look at.
- After Jem has been reading for a while, the kids notice that Mrs. Dubose's frequent corrections of his mistakes had dropped off, and she doesn't even notice when he stops mid-sentence.
- They look at her and, thinking she is in some sort of fit, ask if she's all right, but she doesn't answer.
- Then an alarm clock goes off, and Mrs. Dubose's servant Jessie shoos them out of the house, saying it's time for Mrs. Dubose's medicine.
- They get home at 3:45 and play in the backyard for the rest of the afternoon.
- Atticus comes home bearing gifts, and asks them about their first day at Mrs. Dubose's.

- The days go on for Jem and Scout, and reading to Mrs. Dubose becomes part of their daily schedule.
- One evening Scout asks Atticus what exactly a "nigger-lover" (11.100) is, since that's what Mrs. Dubose frequently calls him, and it's also what Francis said.
- Atticus asks if that's the reason she jumped Francis, and Scout says yes.
- Atticus asks why she's asking if she understood it well enough to make it the reason for a fight, and Scout says that it was the way Francis said it that got on her nerves.
- Atticus tells her that the term doesn't mean anything, but it's something "ignorant, trashy people use [...] when they think somebody's favoring Negroes over and above themselves" (11.107) and that even higher-class people use it sometimes when they want to put someone down.
- When Scout asks, Atticus says that he really is a nigger-lover, because he tries to love everyone. He tells her it's not an insult to the person it's directed at, but instead shows you how "poor" (11.109) the person using it is.
- One afternoon while Jem is plugging away at reading aloud to Mrs. Dubose, Atticus surprises them by coming in.
- It turns out he's just left work – Mrs. Dubose has been setting the alarm clock later and later each day, so Jem and Scout have been staying longer and longer without realizing it.
- Mrs. Dubose says that Jem has to come for a week longer, even though the original month is up, and Atticus says he has to do it.
- During the final week of reading, there's no more alarm clock, but Mrs. Dubose tells them when they can go – and it's usually pretty late when she says so.
- She no longer has fits, but when the book gets boring she amuses herself by picking on the kids – fortunately, Jem's gotten better at not rising to her bait.
- Finally the last day of reading is over, and Jem and Scout are both ecstatic to be free.
- As spring goes on, Jem develops a mastery of what's going on in college football.
- One evening Atticus gets a phone call, and says he's going over to Mrs. Dubose's.
- He comes back with a box, and says that Mrs. Dubose is dead.
- He explains to the kids what's really been going on: Mrs. Dubose was a morphine addict, and she decided she wanted to kick the habit before she died as a matter of personal pride.
- The fits the kids saw her have were caused by withdrawal, and the reading was to keep her mind off the cravings till the alarm clock went off and she could have a dose (which also explains why the reading periods got longer and longer).
- By the end of the reading afternoons, she was free of the drug habit.
- The box Atticus brought home is for Jem, and when he opens it he finds a camellia.
- Jem is angry at this needling from beyond the grave, but Atticus tells him that he thinks it's a message that everything's all right.
- Atticus says that even if Jem hadn't gone on an anti-camellia rampage, Atticus might have made his son go read to Mrs. Dubose anyway, in order "to see what real courage is" (11.153) – not using a gun but fighting for a cause you believe in even if you know you probably won't win.

Chapter Twelve

- Jem's hit the middle school years, and everyone knows what that means: he's angsty, moody, prone to prolonged silences broken by angry outbursts, and thinks Scout should act like a girl.
- Scout asks Atticus and Calpurnia what's up with Jem and whether she can fix it by beating him up, but they say he's just growing up and she should leave him alone.
- Scout decides to hang out with Calpurnia till Dill arrives in Maycomb for the summer, but she gets a letter that Dill's spending some quality time boat-building with his dad, and he's not coming to Maycomb.
- Scout misses Dill horribly – it's not summer without him.
- To make things worse, Atticus (who's a member of the state legislature) gets called into a special session and is away for two weeks.
- With Atticus away, Calpurnia doesn't trust Jem and Scout to go to church by themselves (there was a past incident involving tying up one of their Sunday School classmates in the furnace room), and decides to take them with her to her church instead.
- On Saturday night, Cal scrubs Scout down to her bare skin, and even looks in on an embarrassed Jem's bath.
- Calpurnia also makes sure that there's not a thread out of place on the kids' clothes.
- When Jem asks her why she's being so obsessive about their appearances, she says "I don't want anybody sayin' I don't look after my children" (12.31).
- On Sunday, they head over to First Purchase African M.E. Church outside of town.
- When the Finch kids arrive with Calpurnia, all the men and women already there greet them with respect.
- All, that is, except one – a tall woman named Lula who asks Calpurnia why she's brought white children to the African-American church.
- Jem and Scout feel that they're not wanted, but the crowd, which for a moment seems menacing, drives off Lula and one says that they're glad to have the Finches at their church.
- They enter the church building, which seems plain and ill-equipped compared to their regular church.
- Calpurnia insists on giving Jem and Scout a dime each for the collection, which allows them to keep the dimes Atticus had left them for that purpose.
- Scout asks where the hymn-books are, and Cal says they don't have any, but hushes Scout before she can ask any more questions.
- The priest, Reverend Sykes, begins the service by welcoming the Finches, and then reads some announcements.
- One of the announcements is that the day's collection will go to Helen, Tom Robinson's wife.
- Zeebo leads the congregation in a hymn by reading out each line of the lyrics, which everyone else sings after him, surprising both Scout and Jem, who had never heard of such a thing before.
- Reverend Sykes gives a sermon, which like that of the Finches' usual preacher, focuses on "the Impurity of Women" (12.79).
- Contrary to the Finches' usual church experience, the Reverend names names as to who's been sinning lately, and tells them individually to cut it out.

- After the collection, Jem and Scout are again surprised when Reverend Sykes counts the collection money in front of everyone and then announces they don't have enough – they need at least ten dollars to get Helen and her family through the week.
- The Reverend goes so far as to lock the doors and hold the congregation hostage until they cough up enough cash.
- Jem and Scout put in their dimes from Atticus.
- Once the ten dollars is finally collected, the doors are opened and the service is over.
- Jem and Scout chat with Reverend Sykes, and Scout tries to restrain her curiosity, but can't help asking questions.
- Scout asks the Reverend why Helen's having difficulty finding work, but Calpurnia interrupts before he has a chance to answer.
- Scout asks Calpurnia the same questions, and she says that because of what people say that Tom's done, his family is being shunned.
- Scout presses Calpurnia to tell her what Tom did, and Cal reluctantly tells her that Bob Ewell has accused him of raping Ewell's daughter.
- Scout remembers the Ewells' reputation and wonders why anyone would listen to them, and then asks Calpurnia what rape is, but Cal says she should ask Atticus.
- Jem asks why the congregation sings their hymns the way they do, instead of saving up for hymn-books.
- Cal says that hymn-books wouldn't do them much good – hardly any people in the church can read.
- Cal's one of the few literate ones, as Miss Maudie's aunt, Miss Buford, taught her to read.
- Jem and Scout ask Cal questions about herself, and learn that she's older than Atticus though she doesn't know her age exactly, or even her birthday – she just celebrates it on Christmas to make it easy to remember.
- Cal grew up near Finches' Landing, and moved to Maycomb with Atticus when he married.
- Cal taught Zeebo to read as well, and we find out that Zeebo is her eldest son.
- To teach her son she used the Bible and a book Miss Buford used to teach her – Blackstone's *Commentaries*, a gift from the Finch kids' grandfather.
- Jem's shocked that she's learned and taught English out of such a difficult book as the *Commentaries*, and says that that must be why she doesn't talk like the other African-Americans he knows.
- Scout thinks with wonder that Calpurnia has a whole other life besides being their cook, much like a child realizing that teachers don't sleep at school.
- Jem asks why Cal talked differently at the African-American church than she does with white people, and she says that it makes more sense to fit in.
- Scout asks if she can visit Calpurnia at her home some time, and Cal says yes.
- They arrive home to find Aunt Alexandra installed on their front porch.

Chapter Thirteen

- Scout asks Aunt Alexandra if she's come for a visit, and aunty says that she and Atticus have decided that it's best if she stays with them for a while, as Scout needs some "feminine influence" (13.10).

- Scout does not agree with this, but keeps quiet about it.
- In fact, Scout has trouble making any kind of conversation with her aunt.
- That evening Atticus comes home and confirms Aunt Alexandra's reason for her coming to stay, though Scout thinks it's mostly her aunt's doing, part of her long campaign to do "What Is Best For The Family" (13.22).
- Aunt Alexandra is popular in Maycomb and takes a leading role in the feminine social circles, even though she makes obvious her belief that Finches are superior to everyone else (even though, as Jem says, most people in town are related to the Finches anyhow).
- Aunt Alexandra is a firm believer in Streaks – each family has one (a Drinking Streak, a Gambling Streak, etc.), though Scout doesn't really understand her aunt's obsession with heredity.
- The history of the town, however, suggests that Aunt Alexandra's not totally crazy: its location far away from the river that forms the area's main transportation route means that hardly anyone ever moves to Maycomb or away from it. Because of this, families have known each other for generations, establishing the reputations which Aunt Alexandra refers to as "streaks."
- Scout mostly ignores her aunt, but occasionally gets called in to make an appearance at a luncheon or tea.
- At one such event Scout fails to recognize a woman as her cousin, prompting her aunt to try to instill some family pride into the Finch children.
- Her first attempt is to show them a book their cousin Joshua wrote, but they already know his story from Atticus: he went crazy at college and tried to assassinate the president of the school.
- After this Aunt Alexandra sends Atticus to talk to the kids about being proud of their superior heritage, but he just scares them because he doesn't usually talk to them in that way.
- Scout ends up crying on his lap, and Atticus tells them both to forget it.

Chapter Fourteen

- That incident is enough to make Aunt Alexandra shut up about the Finch Family Pride, just in time for Scout to get some hints that the townspeople are obsessed with the Finch Family Shame.
- After overhearing a passer-by's cryptic comment, Scout asks Atticus what rape is.
- Atticus defines it for her as "carnal knowledge of a female by force and without consent" (14.5)
- Scout doesn't really get what that means, and asks Atticus why Calpurnia wouldn't explain it to her, leading to the story of how Calpurnia took Scout and Jem to her church.
- Aunt Alexandra is none to pleased to find this out, and inserts a resounding "no" into the conversation when Scout asks Atticus if she can visit Calpurnia.
- Scout turns rudely on her aunt for intruding into her conversation with Atticus, but her father makes her apologize.
- Trying to save face, Scout goes to hide in the bathroom, and returns to overhear her aunt

and father quarrelling about an unnamed "her."

- Scout is worried that she's the "her," and feels "the starched walls of a pink cotton penitentiary closing in on" her (14.24).
- Eventually she figures out with relief that it's Calpurnia they're talking about: Alexandra wants to fire her, but Atticus won't hear of it.
- As Scout reenters the room, Aunt Alexandra vents her emotions by stabbing her embroidery angrily.
- Jem pulls Scout out of the room and tells her to try not to get on her aunt's nerves.
- Scout bristles at Jem's assumption that he can tell her what to do and his insistence on talking like he's so much older and wiser than her.
- When he threatens to spank her if she misbehaves again, she flies at him, taking advantage of his weak position to pummel him – her holding her own in the fight, she thinks, shows that they are still equals.
- Atticus comes in and pulls them off each other.
- The siblings become united again when they overhear Aunt Alexandra launching yet another attack on their way of life.
- On the way to bed, Scout steps on something and thinks it's a snake.
- She calls Jem in to investigate, who pokes under her bed with a broom, only to find a very hungry Dill hiding there.
- Dill tells a story (actually two, mutually contradictory stories) about how he escaped from his cruel father and journeyed to Maycomb, and Scout brings him some food.
- Jem breaks the no-tattling rule of childhood and calls in Atticus to tell him about Dill.
- Atticus gets Dill some more food and goes to tell Miss Rachel that her nephew has arrived in Maycomb.
- Scout and Dill hold a grudge against Jem for a short time, but give it up before bedtime.
- After Scout has been asleep for a while, she wakes up to find Dill joining her in bed.
- Scout asks Dill why he ran away, and Dill eventually tells her that he felt like his mom and her new boyfriend weren't paying him any attention and didn't want him around.
- Scout says that her problem is that her family pays her too much attention, but realizes that she would hate it if she didn't feel like they needed her.
- Dill says that he and Scout should get themselves a baby, and tells her a story about where babies come from (no sex is involved in his account), and they slowly drowse off.
- Just before they fall asleep, Scout asks Dill why Boo Radley has never run off, and Dill answers that maybe he doesn't have a place he can run to.

Chapter Fifteen

- It's arranged that Dill can stay in Maycomb for the summer.
- After an uneventful week, one evening Mr. Heck Tate knocks on the front door of the Finch house.
- Jem invites him in, but there's some men in the yard who want Atticus to come out.
- Atticus goes outside, while Jem, Dill, and Scout peer through the windows, to Aunt Alexandra's dismay.
- The bits of the conversation Scout can hear are about Tom Robinson: Tate doesn't want

to keep him in the town jail the night before the trial starts.
- Mr. Link Deas says that Atticus has everything to lose from this case, and Atticus answers, "Do you really think so?" (16.21), which Scout recognizes as his "dangerous question" (16.22), meaning that he's not going to take being messed with.
- Atticus says that whatever happens to Tom, he's going to make sure that the truth gets told.
- When Atticus steps back to the front porch, the men move forward ominously.
- Jem breaks the tension by shouting out that the telephone's ringing, and Atticus tells him to answer it, causing the men – whom Scout now recognizes as people she sees every day – to go off laughing.
- Jem asks if that was a gang, but Atticus says that those were their friends.
- Jem mentions the Ku Klux Klan, but Atticus says that they're gone and will never come back.
- Scout walks Dill home, and returns to find Atticus and Alexandra in the midst of another polite quarrel.
- Scout finds Jem in his room and asks him what's been going on.
- Jem says that Alexandra's been after Atticus about Tom Robinson, and that he (Jem) is afraid something is going to happen to Atticus, but he won't answer any of Scout's questions.
- The next day is Sunday, and Scout seems some men at church who don't usually attend, including Mr. Heck Tate and Mr. Underwood, the editor of *The Maycomb Tribune*.
- Atticus tells Scout that Tom Robinson has arrived at the Maycomb jail, and that they should have kept him there in the first place.
- After church the Finches head back home for a quiet afternoon.
- The evening, however, is marked by a strange event: Atticus comes into the living room with a light bulb and an extension cord. He says that he's going out for a while and won't be back till after the kids are in bed.
- Strange event #2: Atticus takes the car to go wherever he's going, instead of walking like he usually does.
- After bedtime Scout finds Jem getting dressed to go downtown, and Scout insists on going with him and bringing Dill.
- Once they reach the town square, the kids see Atticus's car outside the bank building where his office is, but his light isn't on, so they keep looking for him.
- Finally they see him in front of the jail – a fantastical structure which some people say looks like a Victorian bathroom – reading by the light of the light bulb he went off with.
- Suddenly four cars drive up to the jail, but no one gets out.
- Atticus puts down his newspaper, and Scout thinks that he seems to be expecting these visitors.
- The kids hide in a nearby doorway where they can see and hear what's going on without being seen themselves.
- One man tells Atticus to move away from the door and let them through, but Atticus tells them to go home and that Heck Tate's nearby.
- Another man says that they decoyed Tate out into the woods, and he's not coming back any time soon.
- Atticus says that that changes things, the other man says it does, and Atticus replies once more with "Do you really think so?" (15.89).
- At these words, which she thinks are a signal that something exciting is about to go down,

Scout breaks free of the boys and runs out to Atticus.
- For a moment Atticus looks afraid when he sees Scout, and then again when he sees Jem and Dill.
- Scout looks around and is embarrassed that she doesn't know these men – they're not the same ones as last night.
- Atticus tells Jem to take Scout and Dill home.
- Jem refuses, and father and son face off.
- One of the men grabs Jem, and Scout kicks him in the nuts, making him back off.
- One of the strangers tells Atticus to get rid of the kids, and Atticus pleads with Jem to leave, but Jem isn't budging an inch.
- Scout scans the men for a familiar face, and finally recognizes Mr. Cunningham.
- Scout says hi to Mr. Cunningham and asks him about his entailment, but he doesn't answer.
- Nevertheless, Scout keeps talking to Mr. Cunningham, and tells him that she goes to school with Walter, and to say hi to him for her.
- Scout prattles on about Mr. Cunningham's entailment, remembering past advice from Atticus that it's polite to talk about what other people are interested in, until finally the silence she's met with starts to get to her.
- But then Mr. Cunningham squats down and tells Scout that he's give Walter her message, and then tells the other men that they're going to leave, which they do.
- Scout asks Atticus if they can go home now, and Atticus nods.
- A voice comes from above: Tom Robinson is asking if the men have gone.
- Atticus tells him yes.
- From across the square, another voice: Mr. Underwood has been playing sniper backup from *The Maycomb Tribune* office, where he also lives.
- Atticus and Mr. Underwood talk for a while, and then Atticus and the kids take Atticus's stuff to his car to go home.
- Scout thinks Jem is going to get royally chewed out for following Atticus into town, but she sees her father massaging Jem's hair in affection instead.

Chapter Sixteen

- The night after their run-in at the town jail, Scout ends up sleeping in Jem's room after she starts crying in her own.
- At breakfast the next morning, no one except Jem has much appetite.
- Atticus says he's glad the kids came along, though Aunt Alexandra sniffs that Mr. Underwood would have made sure nothing too bad happened.
- Atticus comments that Mr. Underwood is a strange man – he "despises Negroes" (16.5), yet he acted to protect Atticus and Tom Robinson.
- Scout wants coffee, but Calpurnia will only give her one tablespoon of the evil brew in a cupful of milk.
- Alexandra tells Atticus not to make comments like the one he just made about Mr. Underwood in front of "them" (16.8), i.e. Calpurnia, i.e. African-Americans.
- Atticus says that it's nothing Cal doesn't already know, and that anything that can be said

in table conversation is fit for Calpurnia's ears.

- Alexandra thinks it encourages gossip among the town's African-American residents, and Atticus replies that if the white people didn't do so much that was gossip-worthy the African-Americans wouldn't have so much to talk about.
- Scout asks Atticus why, if Mr. Cunningham is a friend of theirs, he wanted to hurt Atticus last night.
- Atticus says that Mr. Cunningham is a good man, he just has a few "blind spots" (16.18) and he wouldn't have killed him even if Scout hadn't stepped in.
- But Scout's appearance, Atticus continues, made Mr. Cunningham think about what it would be like to be in Atticus's place, and that moment of empathy made him back off.
- As Atticus leaves for the courthouse (telling his kids not to come downtown today), Dill bounces in, saying that the gossip mill is having a field day about how three kids fought off a hundred men with their bare hands.
- Aunt Alexandra steps in on the side of accuracy, but Jem tells her that exaggeration is just how Dill rolls.
- The kids go out to the front porch, and Alexandra tells them to stay inside.
- The porch turns out to be a great lookout point to watch people passing on their way to the courthouse.
- Some of the personalities the kids spot: Mr. Dolphus Raymond, already drunk; a bunch of Mennonites; Mr. Billups whose first name is simply X; Mr. Jake Slade, who's growing his third mouthful of teeth; and the foot-washing Baptists, who pause to shout Bible verses about vanity to Miss Maudie in her revamped yard, who responds in kind.
- The kids head over to Miss Maudie's and ask her if she's going to the courthouse, and she says no, it's too morbid for her.
- That doesn't stop Miss Stephanie Crawford, however, who also stops by on her way, though she doesn't want to admit that the courthouse is where she's going.
- After lunch, when Atticus comes home and tells them that they spent the morning picking the jury, Scout, Jem, and Dill join the crowds at the courthouse.
- Among the strangers the kids spot Mr. Dolphus Raymond, who's drinking out of a paper sack; Jem says that in the bag is a Coca-Cola bottle full of whiskey.
- Dill asks why Mr. Raymond's sitting on the far side of the square with the African-Americans, and Jem says that he likes them better than the whites, and that he has several children by an African-American woman.
- Jem tells more about Mr. Raymond's history: he's from an old, respected family; he was engaged to a white woman, but she shot herself after the wedding rehearsal, perhaps because she found out about his African-American mistress; since then Mr. Raymond's been almost constantly tipsy, but is good to his "mixed" (16.61) children.
- Scout asks what a mixed child is, and Jem tells her that they're biracial, and also that they're "real sad," (16.69), because they don't fully belong on either side of Maycomb's strict racial divide, even when they don't look any different from the other African-Americans.
- Scout says that if you can't tell a person's racial heritage from looking at them, how does Jem know that the Finches are 100% white?
- Jem says that Uncle Jack says that they can't know for certain what happened centuries ago, but that in Maycomb "once you have a drop of Negro blood, that makes you all black" (16.81).
- The lunch break ends and everyone lines up to go back into the courthouse, the

African-Americans letting the white people be at the front of the line.

- Once they get inside the courthouse, Scout gets separated in the rush of people from Jem and Dill.
- Scout overhears some old men saying that Atticus was appointed by the court to defend Tom Robinson, and she wonders why Atticus hadn't told them that – it would have been a convenient excuse in schoolyard brawls.
- By the time the boys find Scout, all the white people are inside the courtroom, and Jem says that there won't be any room left for them.
- Reverend Sykes sees them standing in the lobby and offers to take them up to the balcony (where the African-Americans are segregated).
- Up in the balcony, four people move so that Scout, Jem, Dill, and the Reverend can have front-row seats.
- Scout surveys the scene below her: the jury, made up of farmers (since the townspeople usually got out of jury duty), the lawyers, and the witnesses.
- In charge of the court is Judge Taylor, whose sleepy demeanor conceals an eagle eye, and who has a habit of eating (yes, eating, not smoking) cigars during cases.
- The trial is already in progress, with Mr. Heck Tate on the witness stand.

Chapter Seventeen

- Scout finds Mr. Tate less terrifying in normal clothes.
- The prosecutor, Mr. Gilmer, comes from Abbotsville rather than from Maycomb, and only visits the town for trials.
- Scout finally settles down and starts listening to Mr. Tate's answers to the prosecutor's questions.
- Mr. Tate says that on the night of November 21st Bob Ewell brought him to the Ewell house, where he found Mr. Ewell's daughter, who had been badly beaten. When Mr. Tate asked her who did it, she said Tom Robinson, and when he asked her if Robinson had raped her, she said yes. Then Mr. Tate went and got Robinson, had the Ewell girl identify him, and then arrested him.
- Next, it's Atticus's turn to question the witness. He asks (three times) if Mr. Tate called a doctor to tend to the Ewell girl's injuries, and (all three times) Tate says no. Then he asks Tate to describe those injuries, and he says she had bruises and a black eye. Atticus asks which eye was the black one, and Tate, after giving him a what-kind-of-stupid-question-is-this look, says it was her left. Atticus gets him to clarify that it was the left from his perspective, which means it was the girl's own right. Tate, after another question from Atticus, goes on to describe her injuries further: the right side of her face (where the black eye was) was heavily bruised, and there were finger marks all around her throat.
- That ends Mr. Tate's testimony, and he leaves the witness stand.
- Scout thinks it's all rather boring and dry, not at all the high drama she had expected.
- Bob Ewell is called to the witness stand by his full name, Robert E. Lee Ewell (it's not clear if the E. actually stands for something, or whether it's like Mr. Billups's X).
- Scout thinks about the Ewells: they're always on welfare and they live near an

African-American settlement in a shack behind the dump, which they scavenge.

- Beside the trash and the old cars in their front yard, there's one thing that stands out, or rather six: a set of chipped jars holding well-tended bright red geraniums, which are said to belong to Mayella Ewell.
- Scout remembers a drive past the Ewell place when she went with Atticus to drop off their Christmas tree at the dump: while the nearby African-American houses were warm and inviting, the Ewell residence was not. Scout makes her point clear: "All the little man on the witness stand had that made him any better than his nearest neighbors was, that if scrubbed with lye soap in very hot water, his skin was white" (17.67).
- Mr. Ewell answers the prosecutor's first few questions rudely, until the judge steps in and politely chews him out.
- Mr. Gilmer asks Mr. Ewell to describe what happened that night, and Mr. Ewell does: he came home to hear Mayella screaming inside the house, ran to the window and saw Tom Robinson raping her.
- At his last words the crowd explodes, and Judge Taylor has to bang his gavel for a full five minutes before they calm down.
- Reverend Sykes tells Jem to take Scout and Dill home, but Scout refuses to go and Jem doesn't want to leave, so they all end up staying.
- Mr. Ewell is pleased with the effect he has had on his audience, but Judge Taylor is not.
- The judge says that there's been a request to clear the court, or at least to save the tender ears of the women and children by kicking them out, but that he'll let everyone stay – unless they misbehave, in which case, he'll have them up for contempt of court.
- Mr. Ewell continues his testimony: he ran to get into the house, but the man ran out before he could catch him, so he ran for Mr. Tate.
- Mr. Ewell's so hasty to get off the witness stand that he collides with Atticus, who'd gotten up to question him.
- After Ewell settles back down in the witness chair, Atticus begins his questioning, which begins with the same query he directed at Mr. Tate: whether Ewell called a doctor, or even thought of it. Ewell says no, and furthermore he's never called a doctor for any of his family, as it would cost five dollars.
- Atticus continues by asking Ewell about his daughter's injuries, and he confirms that the sheriff's description was correct.
- The next question Atticus asks is whether Ewell can read and write. The prosecutor objects, but the judge allows Atticus to continue. Ewell answers yes, with a joke about signing his welfare checks that Scout thinks goes over well with the crowd.
- Scout is getting nervous, since she doesn't see where Atticus is heading with these questions.
- Atticus has Ewell write his name, and then states what that action demonstrated: Ewell is left-handed.
- Mr. Gilmer asks Ewell if he's ambidextrous, and the man angrily says no, though he doesn't actually know what the word means.
- Scout notices that Jem is excited, and he whispers that they've got him now, but Scout doesn't see it; Tom Robinson might be left-handed too, and from where she's sitting he certainly looks strong enough to have beaten up Mayella.

Chapter Eighteen

- Mayella Ewell is called to the witness stand.
- Unlike her father, who looked like he had prepared for his appearance in court by bathing for the first time in months if not years, Mayella looks like she actually has an ongoing acquaintance with soap and water.
- Mr. Gilman asks Mayella to describe what happened that night in her own words, but she doesn't answer, so he switches to more specific questions.
- Her answers are still minimal, so the judge asks her to just tell the court what happened, and she bursts into tears.
- Judge Taylor tells her that she has no cause for shame or fear, so long as she tells the truth.
- The judge asks Mayella what she's scared of, and she points to Atticus.
- When the judge asks Mayella how old she is, she says nineteen and a half.
- The judge tells Mayella that Mr. Finch isn't going to scare her, and that his job as judge is to stop him if he tries.
- Mayella, soothed, finally gets going on her testimony.
- What she says: she was on the porch when Tom Robinson came by, she asked him to chop up an old piece of furniture for kindling, and when she went inside to get a nickel to pay him he attacked her from behind.
- Mr. Gilmer asks if she screamed and fought back, and she says yes.
- Mr. Gilmer asks her what happened next, and she says she can't really remember, but eventually her father and Mr. Tate were there.
- Mr. Gilmer asks again if Mayella tried to fight off her attacker, and if he took "full advantage" (18.38) of her, and she answers yes to both questions.
- Mr. Gilmer sits down, and Atticus stands up to question the witness.
- Mayella takes offense to Atticus's calling her "ma'am" (she thinks he's making fun of her), and Scout wonders what her life is like that she thinks normal courtesy is rudeness.
- Atticus asks Mayella about herself: she's the eldest of seven kids, her mom's been dead for a while, she can read and write but she only went to school for two or three years.
- Then Atticus asks Mayella if she has any friends, and again she thinks he's making fun, since the idea seems so absurd to her.
- Atticus asks Mayella about her father (who's still in the room), whether he's ever beaten her, and she says, after a hesitation, that he's never touched her.
- Finally Atticus's questions turn to the day of the alleged crime; Mayella says that Tom passed the house every day, but this was the first time she had asked him to come into the yard (though she jumped when he asked that question), though she might have asked him to do odd jobs before, she can't remember.
- Atticus quotes Mayella's previous testimony and asks her whether the defendant hit her face; she says no, then yes, then that she can't remember, then cries.
- When asked to identify the man who raped her, Mayella indicates Tom, but Atticus tells him to stand up so that Mayella can have a good look at him.
- Tom stands up, revealing that his left arm is a foot shorter than his right and his left hand is shriveled.
- Up in the balcony, Reverend Sykes tells Jem and Scout that Tom caught his hand in a cotton gin when he was a boy.

- Atticus asks Mayella how this man could have raped her, and she says she doesn't know how it happened but it did.
- Mr. Gilmer objects that Atticus is browbeating the witness.
- Judge Taylor replies that if anyone's doing any browbeating it's Mayella, but he's the only one laughing at his joke, as the rest of the courtroom is completely silent.
- Atticus asks Mayella if she wants to reconsider any of her testimony, but she sticks to her story, adding some new details to try to make it make more sense.
- Atticus asks a series of questions that Mayella simply refuses to answer: why the other children didn't hear her screams, if she screamed when she saw her father in the window instead of at Tom, if her father was the one who beat her up.
- After meeting all these questions with silence, Mayella makes her final statement: "That nigger yonder took advantage of me an' if you fine fancy gentlemen don't wanta do nothin' about it then you're all yellow stinkin' cowards" (18.167).
- After that Mayella bursts into tears and refuses to answer any more questions, whether from Atticus, from Mr. Gilmer, or from Judge Taylor himself.
- Scout thinks that somehow Atticus had wounded Mayella in a way Scout doesn't understand, and that it made Atticus sick to do it.
- Mayella leaves the witness stand, directing a dagger-look of hatred at Atticus on the way.
- The lawyers whisper together and then leave the courtroom, and the audience takes a stretch break.
- Mr. Underwood sees Jem, Scout, and Dill among the African-Americans in the balcony.
- Scout wonders about the nuances of the case she might be missing, since it all seems fairly straightforward to her, and remembers that Atticus told her that Judge Taylor is a good judge.
- The judge and the lawyers return to restart the case.
- Jem, Scout, and Dill are pleased to see that the Judge has brought a cigar with him, which he proceed to begin eating, spitting out the bits once he chews them up.
- It's now almost 4 p.m., and Judge Taylor asks Atticus if they can finish the case up this afternoon.
- Atticus says he thinks they can, and he has just one witness to call.

Chapter Nineteen

- Tom Robinson tries to use his good right hand to put his bad left one on the Bible, but it keeps falling off, and the judge tells him not to bother.
- After the basic questions about his age and family, Atticus asks Tom about a previous conviction for disorderly conduct; Jem whispers that Atticus is showing the jury that Tom has nothing to hide.
- Tom's testimony continues: as Mayella said, he passes the Ewell place on his way to work for Mr. Link Deas every day because there's no other way to get there; he did go inside the Ewell yard to chop up a piece of furniture, but that was last spring, not in November like Mayella said, and that he went home without incident after turning down the nickel she offered him for the job.
- Atticus asks if he ever crossed into Ewell property after that, and Tom says he did lots of

times, provoking a murmur from the audience.
- Atticus asks why, and Tom says Mayella kept having little jobs for him to do, and he never took payment because he knew how poor she was.
- Tom says the children were always hanging around when he was there, and that Mayella would talk to him.
- Scout thinks that Mayella must have been terribly lonely, even more lonely than Boo Radley, and that Tom was probably the only person who had ever treated her with real kindness.
- Atticus asks if Tom ever went on the Ewell property without being invited, and he says no – and Scout believes him.
- Atticus asks Tom about that night in November, and Tom describes his memory of what happened: he was going home as usual, passed the Ewell place which seemed quieter than usual; Mayella, sitting on the front porch, asked him to come in to fix a door; when he looked at the door, nothing seemed wrong with it; he suddenly realized that the reason it seemed so quiet was that the other children weren't around; he asked where they were, and she said she had been saving her nickels for a year to get enough money for all seven to buy ice cream; he said it was a good thing for her to treat them, and that if there was nothing for him to do that he'd be leaving; then she asked him to get something down from the top of a wardrobe; he stood on a chair to get it, when she grabbed his legs from behind; he jumped in fright, knocking the chair over, which he swears was the only furniture disturbed in the room when he left it.
- Atticus asks Tom what happened next, and the defendant pauses nervously, causing the judge to tell him to answer the question.
- Tom says that he turned around and Mayella hugged him, and the Judge bangs his gavel to restore order as the lights go on in the courtroom to counter the gathering dusk.
- Tom continues: Mayella kissed him, saying that she'd never kissed an adult man before, and that her father does to her doesn't count, and told Tom to kiss her back.
- Tom says that he told Mayella to move out of his way so he could leave, since he didn't want to push her out of the way to get by her, when Mr. Ewell shouted through the window.
- Atticus forces Tom to repeat Mr. Ewell's words, even though he doesn't want to: he said, "you goddamn whore, I'll kill ya" (19.68).
- Tom says that after that he just ran away as fast as he could, and never laid a finger on Mayella.
- Scout thinks that Tom's manners are, in their way, as good as her father's, but she doesn't understand Tom's dilemma until her father explains it to her later: pushing Mayella would have been as good as signing his death warrant, so he had to run, even though it made him look guilty.
- Atticus asks Tom if Mr. Ewell said anything to him, and Tom said if he did he was running so fast he didn't hear it, but it seemed to him that the man's attention was on his daughter.
- Atticus asks Tom why he ran, and he says it was because he was scared.
- Atticus sits down, and while Mr. Gilmer is getting up to question the witness, Mr. Link Deas suddenly stands up and vouches for Tom's character to the whole courtroom, sparking Judge Taylor's wrath.
- The judge tells everyone to forget the interruption and the court reporter to erase it from the record, and the case continues.
- After revisiting Tom's previous criminal record, Mr. Gilmer asks him about his physical

strength, establishing that after all he's strong enough to chop up furniture with his one good hand.

- Mr. Gilmer asks why Tom spent so much time doing Mayella's chores when he had his own to do at home, and Tom says, after persistent questioning, that he felt sorry for her.
- Mr. Gilmer shows shock and horror at this answer (how dare a black man feel sorry for a white woman?), and pauses to let the jury feel it too.
- Mr. Gilmer's questions turn to the evening of the alleged crime; Tom refuses to accuse Mayella of lying, but persistently says that she is "mistaken in her mind" (19.135).
- While Mr. Gilmer tries to make Tom's running away from the scene of the supposed crime into evidence of his guilt, Tom holds fast to saying that he ran basically because he knew most white people would assume he was guilty no matter what.
- By this point Dill is crying uncontrollably, and Jem makes Scout take him out of the courtroom.
- The two children go outside, and Dill tells Scout it just made him sick to hear how Mr. Gilmer was talking to Tom.
- Scout says he's just doing his job, but Dill says there's a difference between the condescending way Mr. Gilmer talked to Tom and the politeness Atticus showed to Mayella.
- Scout replies that the difference is between Atticus and Mr. Gilmer, not their witnesses, but Dill doesn't believe it.
- A new voice breaks into their conversation: Mr. Dolphus Raymond, who agrees with Dill.

Chapter Twenty

- Mr. Raymond offers Dill his paper bag, which worries Scout, but Dill says it's nothing worse than Coca-Cola.
- Mr. Raymond asks the kids not to give away his secret – he just pretends to drink all the time because it gives other people an excuse when he does things they don't like, keeping them from giving up on him altogether.
- Scout says that the way he acts isn't honest, but Mr. Raymond says that other people will never understand that he lives the way he does because he likes it, but drunken stupidity they do understand.
- Scout asks why he's told them his secret, and he says it's because they're kids and they know better than their elders – Dill's crying shows that the world hasn't gotten hold of him and made him blind to its meanness.
- Scout says Atticus sees it too, but Mr. Raymond says he's an unusual case, and all you have to do is look back inside the courthouse to see how unusual.
- This reminds Scout that she's missing out on the trial, and while talking to Mr. Raymond is tempting, the courtroom calls her back.
- Dill and Scout return to the balcony, where Reverend Sykes has saved them seats, to find Atticus already halfway through his closing remarks.
- Scout asks Jem to fill her in, and Jem says Atticus has just gone over the evidence and there's no way they can lose.
- Atticus, after asking permission from the judge, takes off his coat, unbuttons his vest and

collar, and loosens his tie – shocking his children, who have never, ever before seen him so undressed outside of his bedroom.
- Atticus's tone of voice loosens its buttons too, becoming conversational rather than businesslike.
- What he says to the jury: the case shouldn't have even come to trial, because the prosecution doesn't have any medical evidence that sex, let alone rape, took place; Mayella's accusations are motivated by guilt over her desire for Tom Robinson; Mayella was beaten by a man who led with his left, and Mr. Ewell is left-handed while Tom most decidedly is not; the witnesses for the prosecution testified with the attitude that as whites they would be believed while Tom, as an African-American, would not; the notion that the prosecution's witnesses are banking on is that all African-Americans are immoral liars who rape white women whenever they get the chance, but the jury is smart enough to see that for the lie it is, and to know that African-Americans are no worse than any other race.
- At this point Scout notices another first: Atticus is sweating.
- Atticus continues to the jury: he cites Thomas Jefferson's famous line that all men are created equal, and says that this doesn't mean that everyone is just as talented as everyone else, but that everyone is equal under the law.
- He ends his speech with a plea to the jury: "In the name of God, do your duty" (20.52).
- Atticus turns to go back to his seat, softly saying something else that Scout doesn't hear; she asks Jem, and he says that Atticus said "In the name of God, believe him" (20.54).
- Then Jem and Scout are dismayed to see Calpurnia making a beeline up the center aisle of the courtroom towards Atticus.

Chapter Twenty-One

- Calpurnia waits for the judge to see her and then asks permission to give Atticus a note.
- The judge says it's okay; Atticus reads the note tells the judge that it's from his sister and says that his children are missing.
- Mr. Underwood speaks up and tells Atticus they're in the balcony and have been there all afternoon.
- Atticus tells the kids to come down from there, and they do.
- Atticus sends the kids home with Calpurnia and at first tells them to stay there, but after some strategic whining he agrees that they can come back once they've had their dinner.
- All they way home Cal chews Jem out for bringing his sister into the trial, and Scout is pleased that Jem's been knocked off the pedestal she thinks he's always occupied in Cal's eyes.
- Jem, still riding the euphoria of thinking they're going to win the case, doesn't care.
- Aunt Alexandra is ready to faint from horror when she hears where they've been.
- After dinner the kids make it back to the courthouse to find the loyal Reverend Sykes has still saved their seats for them.
- Scout and Jem are surprised that hardly anyone has left – usually everyone heads out once the jury leaves to deliberate.
- They talk to Reverend Sykes about the formalities that happened while they were gone.
- Jem says that they've won the case, but the Reverend says that he's never seen a jury

support an African-American man over a white one.
- The court audience waits patiently for the jury to come to a verdict – like they were in church, Scout thinks.
- After three hours of this, Scout drowses off for a bit, and wakes up thinking about the morning when Atticus shot the mad dog.
- Mr. Tate calls the court to order and brings Tom Robinson back into the room.
- The jury comes in, and announces their unanimous verdict: guilty.
- Atticus whispers something to Tom Robinson, packs up his papers, and leaves.
- As he walks down the aisle alone, the African-Americans in the balcony silently stand up to honor him.

Chapter Twenty-Two

- Jem can't hold back the injustice-fueled tears as he, Scout, and Dill go to meet Atticus outside the courthouse.
- He says to Atticus that it's not right, and Atticus agrees.
- Aunt Alexandra is waiting up for them when they get home (still wearing her corset even under her bathrobe, Scout thinks), and tells Atticus she's sorry he lost the case.
- Even slightly softened, Alexandra doesn't miss the chance to remind Atticus that she doesn't think he should have let the kids listen in on the case.
- Atticus says that they have to deal with the fallout from it anyway, and that racism is just as much a Maycomb standby as missionary teas are.
- Atticus goes to bed wearily, but seems more hopeful in the morning.
- At breakfast he tells his family that it's not over yet – there's still the appeal process.
- Breakfast is a lavish affair, as it seems every African-American in the county has sent the Finches a gift of food.
- Calpurnia says she found everything on the back steps when she arrived that morning, and asks if they were overstepping themselves; Atticus, a bit teary-eyed, tells her to thank everyone but tell them that there's no need to be so generous, especially when times are so hard.
- Atticus leaves for town, and his place at the breakfast table is taken by Dill.
- The kids soon head out themselves, and see Miss Stephanie Crawford giving a blow-by-blow account of the trial to Miss Maudie Atkinson and Mr. Avery.
- Miss Maudie calls Jem over; Miss Stephanie butts in to pepper them with rude questions, before Miss Maudie shuts her up and offers the kids some cake.
- There are two little cakes and one big one, and Scout thinks that Miss Maudie has uncharacteristically forgotten Dill, but then finds out the big cake is for Jem.
- Scout realizes this is Miss Maudie's way of saying everything is still cool between them.
- Miss Maudie tells them that some men just get stuck with the sucky jobs, and Atticus is unfortunately one of them.
- Jem says that he always thought that Maycomb folks were good people, but it doesn't seem like that to him any more, since no one stepped up to support Tom Robinson.
- Miss Maudie said that some did, including Judge Taylor, who usually appoints an inexperienced local lawyer as public defender, but made an exception in Tom Robinson's

case to appoint Atticus instead.
- Miss Maudie goes on to say that she knew Atticus wouldn't win, but that he made the jury think about their decision for a long time, and that's a baby step in the right direction.
- They leave Miss Maudie's house, and Dill says that he's going to be a clown when he grows up, because the only possible response to humanity is to laugh at it.
- Jem says that Dill's got it wrong, clowns get laughed at by everyone else, but Dill says he'll be a new sort of clown who looks at the audience and laughs at them.
- Miss Rachel and Aunt Alexandra tell the kids to get off the street, there's trouble coming, and Miss Stephanie butts in to tell them why: that morning Mr. Ewell spit in Atticus's face and told him that he had it out for him.

Chapter Twenty-Three

- Atticus won't say much about the attack other than to joke about it with dry wit.
- Scout thinks Atticus should carry a gun, but he responds with calm unconcern.
- Finally Atticus figures out that his kids are really terrified that Mr. Ewell will follow through on his threat, but Atticus thinks that Ewell's done as much as he's going to do, and after that the kids don't feel scared any more.
- Atticus tells Jem and Scout that nothing can happen to Tom until the appeal, which might have a better result than the original trial.
- Tom is now at the Enfield Prison Farm seventy miles away, where his family can't visit him.
- Scout asks what will happen to Tom if he loses his appeal, and Atticus says he'll go to the electric chair unless the governor grants him a stay of execution.
- Jem says it's not fair for Tom to get the death penalty since he didn't kill anyone, and that the jury could have given him a prison sentence instead.
- Atticus says that no Southern jury would convict an African-American man on a rape charge and give him anything less than death.
- Jem replies that maybe rape shouldn't be punishable by death then.
- Atticus says that he doesn't disagree with the sentencing recommendations for rape, but his beef is with sentencing a man to death on purely circumstantial evidence.
- He goes on to say that the law requires a reasonable doubt to acquit someone, but he thinks that a shadow of a doubt should be enough – as long as there's the possibility that the accused is innocent.
- Jem then says that it's the jury's fault, and that maybe they should just get rid of juries.
- Atticus answers that it would be better to change the law so that only judges could inflict the death penalty.
- Jem thinks that's a good idea, and tells Atticus he should make it happen, but Atticus says changing laws, like breaking up, is hard to do.
- Jem still thinks that juries are a crock of @#$%, and Atticus tells him that if the jury had been made up of Jem and others like him, Tom would have been acquitted. He goes on to say that the jury left behind the written law to follow the unwritten one – that the white man always wins.
- Atticus tells Jem and Scout that throughout their lives they'll see plenty of instances of

white men cheating black ones, but that any white man who does so is nothing more than trash.

- He continues with an ominous prediction: "Don't fool yourselves – it's all adding up and one of these days we're going to pay the bill for it" (23.41).
- Jem asks why none of the townspeople like Miss Maudie ever get drafted for jury duty.
- Atticus says that women aren't allowed to be on juries, and that the rest either don't want to lose business by taking sides, or are just to scared to stake out a definite position on an issue when so much depends on it.
- Jem says that this particular jury didn't waste any time staking out its position, but Atticus disagrees – like Miss Maudie, he thinks that the few hours the jury was out shows that the world might be shifting a little bit in the right direction.
- Despite the supposed secrecy of jury deliberations, Atticus knows who kept the jury from convicting Tom right away: a cousin of Mr. Walter Cunningham, part of the group who wanted to lynch Tom when he was in the Maycomb jail the night before the trial but was turned back by Scout.
- Scout decides to make friends with the younger Walter Cunningham when school starts up again, but Aunt Alexandra decrees that that Cunninghams are one class and the Finches another, and never the twain shall meet.
- Scout remembers that Aunty reacted the same way when she wanted to visit Calpurnia at home, and decides not to give in so easily this time.
- Aunt Alexandra finally says that the Cunninghams are trash and she doesn't want Scout to pick up any more bad habits; at this Scout is ready to explode, but Jem gets her out of the room before she can jump on Aunt Alexandra.
- Jem gives Scout a Tootsie Roll to calm her down (or at least shut her up by giving her a mouthful to chew on), and Scout notices that Jem looks different – he's growing up.
- Jem tries to show off his new chest hair; even though Scout can't see anything, but she doesn't tell him so.
- Jem tells Scout that she shouldn't let Aunt Alexandra annoy her, and Scout remembers when his advice was the other way around, and it was she who shouldn't annoy Aunty.
- Jem asks Scout if she can't take up some kind of girly occupation to make Aunt Alexandra feel better, but Scout says she doesn't want to and she doesn't care what Aunty thinks.
- Scout goes on to say that it wasn't Aunt Alexandra's comments about her that set her off, but her calling Walter trash, which she thinks puts him down to the level of the Ewells.
- Jem says that he thinks he's got it figured out, and there are four kinds of people: the ordinary (the Finches and their neighbors), the ones who live in the woods (the Cunninghams), the ones who live by the dump (the Ewells), and the African Americans, and everyone hates the ones a step below them.
- Scout doesn't quite buy it, and the pair try to puzzle out why Aunt Alexandra is so hung up on the notion of Family.
- Scout finally concludes that people are just people and that's all there is to it, and Jem says that's what he used to think, but if it's true, why can't we all just get along?
- The confusing way people act makes Jem think he finally understands why Boo Radley never comes out – because he wants to stay in, away from the weirdness that is humankind.

Chapter Twenty-Four

- It's the end of August, and Aunt Alexandra is hosting a missionary tea at the Finch house.
- Unusually, she's letting Calpurnia serve, rather than controlling every detail like she usually does.
- Doubly unusually, Scout is indoors – Jem is occupied in teaching Dill to swim, and they're skinny-dipping so they won't let her come along.
- Aunt Alexandra had told Scout to come in when they were having refreshments, but Scout knows that if she gets her dress dirty Cal will have to wash it on top of her tea-related chores, so she decides the kitchen is safer.
- Scout offers to help Calpurnia serve, and gets to carry in the silver coffee pitcher.
- Aunt Alexandra, pleased that the pink-dressed Scout managed to carry something without spilling it, asks her to join them.
- Scout feels her usual nervousness in the presence of a group of ladies, and decides not to speak until spoken to.
- Miss Stephanie Crawford asks Scout if she wants to be a lawyer when she grows up; Scout says no, and tries to think of what she does want to be.
- Miss Stephanie, in her needling way, says she would have thought Scout would choose the law, since she's already taken to attending trials.
- Miss Stephanie, encouraged by the general laughter that her remark sets off, asks Scout again if she wants to be a lawyer.
- Miss Maudie puts her hand on Scout's, and Scout replies that she doesn't want to be a lawyer, just a lady.
- Miss Stephanie, suspecting she's being poked back but not sharply enough for her to be able to take offense, says that Scout will have to get used to wearing dresses if she wants to succeed.
- Miss Maudie holds Scout's hand more tightly, and Scout wisely keeps her mouth shut.
- Scout takes up conversation with Mrs. Grace Merriweather, who had reported to the group on the Mruna tribe, whom J. Grimes Everett is trying to convert to Christianity.
- J. Grimes Everett's saintly behavior is apparently Mrs. Merriweather's favorite topic, and she goes on about him at great length.
- Eventually Mrs. Merriweather is distracted by a conversation going on next to her
- She makes a comment about the need to "forgive and forget," and to help an unknown woman "lead a Christian life for those children from here on out" (24.36).
- Scout asks if she's talking about Mayella Ewell, but Mrs. Merriweather says no, she's talking about Helen Robinson (though she doesn't actually know the woman's name).
- Mrs. Merriweather talks about how distressing it is when the colored help is cranky about something, and how it's important to remind them that Jesus was never cranky about anything so they should strive to do the same.
- Mrs. Farrow replies that there's nothing white people can do to change the inherent immoral nature of the black man.
- Mrs. Merriweather continues that she won't name names, but there are some "good but misguided" (24.47) people in Maycomb who think they're helping but are really just making trouble.
- Miss Maudie breaks in to say, "His food doesn't stick going down, does it?" (24.48), and a daydreaming Scout can tell she's very angry, though she doesn't understand why.

- Aunt Alexandra smoothes things over with more cake, and turns the conversation in less dangerous directions, while also shooting Miss Maudie a thank-you look which Scout notices but again does not understand.
- Scout wonders if she'll ever be able to function in this world of ladies whose rules make so little sense to her, especially compared to the male world.
- Apparently while Scout has been musing on gender the conversation has turned back to race, for she tunes in just in time to hear Mrs. Merriweather saying that white people who don't believe in segregation are hypocrites.
- Scout tunes out again to think about what Calpurnia had told her about Tom Robinson: that ever since he went to prison, he's just given up hoping he'll ever be free.
- Atticus comes home earlier than usual, and he's not looking too good.
- He asks Aunt Alexandra to come to the kitchen with him so they can talk to Calpurnia, and Miss Maudie and Scout follow them.
- Atticus tells them all that Tom Robinson is dead – he tried to climb over the prison fence right in front of the guards and was shot, no fewer than seventeen times.
- Atticus asks Calpurnia to come with him to break the news to Helen.
- After they leave, a stunned Aunt Alexandra and Miss Maudie sit in the kitchen with Scout.
- Aunt Alexandra is worried about the effect all this strain is having on Atticus's health, and mad at the town that puts the responsibility of doing the right thing on his shoulders because they're too scared to do it themselves.
- Miss Maudie says that "the handful of people in this town with background" (24.81) share the principles he's working to uphold, and are grateful to Atticus for fighting on the side of the angels.
- Aunt Alexandra composes herself and they go back in to face the tea party, acting as if nothing is wrong, and Scout joins them in their effort to keep up a ladylike attitude.

Chapter Twenty-Five

- September has arrived, but autumn coolness hasn't, so Scout and Jem are still sleeping out on the back porch.
- There Scout finds a roly-poly bug, and amuses herself by poking it so it rolls up, waiting for it to unroll and start walking, then poking it again.
- She's about to squish it when Jem stops her, and she makes fun of him for being so sympathetic towards bugs.
- Scout thinks that Jem is the one who's getting more like a girl, not her.
- Dill has gone back to Meridian for the school year, and thinking about Dill sends Scout onto thinking about what Dill told her before he left town.
- Cue memory flashback: On the day of the missionary tea, Jem and Dill had been walking back from the swimming hole trying to hitch a ride when they saw Atticus driving somewhere with Calpurnia.
- Atticus wanted them to try to get another ride since he wasn't going to go home for a while, but the boys convinced him to let them come with him.
- As they drove to the Robinson house, Atticus told them what had happened to Tom.
- When they arrived, Mrs. Robinson was out, so one of her kids went to bring her back.

- When Mrs. Robinson saw that Atticus had bad news, she fainted.
- Atticus and Calpurnia brought Mrs. Robinson into the house and stayed with her for some time, while the boys waited in the car as Atticus had asked them to do.
- Calpurnia stayed with the Robinson while Atticus drove the boys home.
- As they passed the Ewell place, they heard voices shouting at them, but Dill couldn't tell what they were saying. And that's the end of Dill's story of that day.
- Tom's death is the hot topic in Maycomb gossip for a few days, mostly as a way to reinforce pre-existing stereotypes as to the foolishness of black people.
- The story seems well on its way to dying a quick death until Mr. Underwood comes out with an editorial on the topic in *The Maycomb Tribune* – since it's the only paper in town, he can say whatever he want and not lose subscribers or advertising, though he doesn't really care if he does.
- Mr. Underwood is furious and he's not going to take it anymore, so he's written a blistering editorial about how even though on the surface it seemed that Tom had due process of law, internal racism meant that he was doomed from the moment Mayella screamed.
- Miss Stephanie, ever the joyful bearer of bad news, tells Aunt Alexandra and Jem that when Mr. Ewell heard of Tom's death, he said one down, two to go.
- Jem passes this on to Scout, but tells her not to worry, and also, under pain of serious silent treatment from him, not to even hint that she knows what Ewell said to Atticus.

Chapter Twenty-Six

- School starts – third grade for Scout and seventh for Jem – so once again they're passing the Radley Place every day; though it's not as frightening as it used to be, it's still dreary-looking.
- Jem is excited about his place on the football team, even though they won't let him do much beyond carrying buckets.
- Scout feels a little sorry for all the annoyance they must have caused in the old days trying to get Boo to show his face.
- But Scout still remembers the gifts he left for them in the tree, and keeps an eye out for him each time she goes by the house.
- Scout mentions to Atticus that she'd still like to set eyes on Boo Radley sometime, and he tells her to cut it out, and mentions the time they almost got shot in the Radley yard – the first time he's let on that he knows what really happened that night, which seems so long ago to Scout now.
- Boo Radley seems positively tame after the events of the last year; Scout's still worried about the blowback from the Robinson case, but Atticus thinks that time will bring forgetfulness.
- Forgetfulness is long in coming, however, and Jem and Scout are practicing their gentleman and lady skills in the schoolyard, where most of their classmates share their parents' prejudices.
- Scout wonders why if everyone disagrees with Atticus they still re-elected him to represent them in the state government, and concludes that people are just plain weird.

- Every week, Scout's class has a Current Events assignment: kids are supposed to report on an article from a newspaper, except the poor kids don't have access to newspapers, except one they call The Grit Paper which the teacher doesn't deem acceptable for the assignment.
- Even the town kids have problems with the assignment, though: one reports on an advertisement instead of an article, while another starts out calling Hitler "Old Adolf."
- Miss Gates, the teacher, seizes on the moment to teach her about the difference between democracy and dictatorship, and about the persecution of Jews.
- When Miss Gates switches from Hitler to arithmetic, Scout thinks about her father's dislike of Hitler.
- Later she asks him why the people Hitler's persecuting don't just persecute him instead, since there's lots of them and only one Hitler, and Atticus answers that he doesn't know.
- Scout asks Atticus if hating Hitler is okay, and he tells her that hating people is never okay, even if it's Hitler.
- Scout still can't quite formulate the question that's bugging her, so she goes to Jem, who's eaten his way through several bunches of bananas in an attempt to bulk up so he can play on the football team.
- Scout tries to explain what's bothering her: it's bad to persecute people, and Miss Gates seems really upset at the way Hitler's persecuting the Jews, but she remembers Miss Gates coming down the courthouse steps after the trial saying "it's time somebody taught them a lesson" (26.56).
- Scout finally figures out her question: "how can you hate Hitler so bad an' then turn around and be ugly about folks right at home[?]" (26.56).
- Jem interrupts her before she can finish and tells her never to mention the courthouse to him again.
- Scout goes back to Atticus and tries to climb in his lap, though she doesn't really fit there any more.
- Atticus says he heard her conversation with Jem, and that she shouldn't let her brother's crabbiness get her down – he's still trying to process what happened with Tom Robinson, and once he gets through it he'll be all right.

Chapter Twenty-Seven

- By the middle of October, things in Maycomb have mostly settled down.
- Mr. Ewell gets a job with the WPA, but gets fired for laziness – a feat Scout has never heard of before or since (historical context note: the Works Progress Administration was created to give unemployed people jobs during the Depression, and a person would have to be a really bad worker to get fired by them).
- After that Mr. Ewell goes back to picking up his weekly welfare check while blaming Atticus for his unemployment, frightening the welfare lady enough that she warns Atticus, but he tells her not to worry.
- Meanwhile, one Sunday night while his wife is away at church, Judge Taylor hears a scratching noise at the back of his house, and his wife comes home to find him holding his shotgun on his lap.

- Around the same time, Mr. Link Deas gives Helen a job, even though he doesn't have much for her to do.
- Eventually Mr. Deas finds out that Helen has to go a mile in the wrong direction to avoid the Ewells, who harass her every time she walks by their place, so over Helen's protestations he walks her home one day.
- On his way back he stops at the strangely silent Ewell place, and shouts that if he hears about them causing Helen any more trouble they'll be in jail so fast they won't have time to shut the door behind them.
- The next day, Mr. Ewell follows Helen to work, and Mr. Deas chews him out again; after that the Ewells don't bother her any more.
- Aunt Alexandra is worried by these signs that Mr. Ewell is not one to forgive and forget, but Atticus tells her not to worry, he'll get over it soon.
- After these incidents, life goes on as usual for Scout.
- As the end of October approaches, Scout remembers what happened the previous Halloween: the local kids get up a prank on two deaf old ladies, taking all the furniture out of their house and hiding it in their cellar.
- The ladies insist on bloodhounds to track down their stolen property, and Mr. Tate obliges, though he has to travel ten miles to get them.
- After three failed tries to get the bloodhounds to find a trail leading away from the house, Mr. Tate finally realized what had happened.
- Once news gets out of his discovery, wearing shoes becomes a sudden fashion for the Maycomb kids, and no one goes barefoot until the hounds are out of town.
- This year, the Maycomb ladies are determined to keep the kids out of trouble, so they've planned a carnival in the high school auditorium.
- Jem and Scout are dismayed at this attempt to impose adult order on Halloween, but Scout plans to attend the carnival anyway.
- Scout soon finds herself pressed into service to play a ham in Mrs. Grace Merriweather's tribute to Maycomb agriculture.
- Mrs. Crenshaw makes Scout a ham costume out of wire and cloth, which is convincing if constricting.
- Neither Atticus nor Aunt Alexandra has the energy to attend the parade of meats, so Scout gives them a preview in the living room and gets Jem to take her over to the high school.

Chapter Twenty-Eight

- It's a warm but windy moonless evening as Jem and Scout walk from their house to the high school, Jem carrying Scout's ham costume.
- The kids joke about haints, which no longer seem scary now that they're so grown up.
- They pass by the Radley Place, and pause to listen for a moment, but all is silent except for a solitary mockingbird.
- They turn through a field to reach the school, feeling their way around an oak tree through the pitch-black darkness.
- Someone leaps out at them with a light, scaring them half to death, but it turns out to be only Cecil Jacobs.

- Cecil tells Scout he's left his cow costume behind the stage, and Scout can do the same with her ham; Jem is glad that Scout has someone her own age to hang out with and won't be tagging along with him.
- They arrive at the crowded auditorium, and Cecil and Scout go to drop off the ham costume, then see the sights.
- Soon the kids gather for the pageant, and Scout wriggles into her ham costume, now slightly mashed.
- Mrs. Merriweather reads her pageant narration, which gives in great detail the history of Maycomb County.
- Scout, seeing that it's going to go on for a while, takes a nap inside her ham costume, and misses her cue.
- To make matters worse, when Scout finally gets onstage it's the middle of the finale, and later Mrs. Merriweather scolds her for ruining the pageant.
- Jem talks to Scout to make her feel better, and Scout thinks he's getting as good at it as Atticus.
- Scout doesn't want to face anyone after her mess-up, so she and Jem wait until the audience has gone, and Scout keeps her ham costume on, the better to hide from everyone.
- They leave the school to go back the way they came, through the midnight-black field.
- Scout realizes she's forgotten her shoes, but when they turn back to get them the lights at the school go off, and Jem tells her she'll have to go back tomorrow.
- Jem seems nervous about something, and tells Scout to shush for a while.
- Scout tells him she's too old to play these games, but Jem tells her he hears something when they're walking, but it stops when they do.
- Jem says it's probably just Cecil, and they keep walking.
- Scout asks how Cecil can see them in the darkness, and Jem says that the fat streaks in her ham are made with reflective paint.
- Scout shouts a teasing comment at Cecil Jacobs, but doesn't get any response; odd, she thinks, for Cecil to delay the payoff of a prank for so long.
- Jem asks Scout if she can take off her costume, and she says she thinks so, but she's not wearing much under it.
- Jem says he has Scout's dress, but she says she can't put it on in the dark.
- Scout realizes that Jem knows it's not Cecil, but he's pretending he thinks it is so as not to scare her.
- When they reach the oak tree they pause for a moment, but their stalker doesn't stop – he runs towards them, and they can tell it's not a kid who's been following them.
- Jem screams at Scout to run, but she's off-kilter in her ham costume.
- Something knocks into her and she falls to the ground.
- Scout hears Jem fighting with someone, but can't see who it is.
- Jem breaks free, grabs Scout, and runs for the road, but something pulls him back.
- Scout hears more fighting, then a crunch and a scream from Jem.
- Scout runs back towards Jem and crashes into a man's stomach.
- The man squeezes her until she can barely breathe, but suddenly falls backwards; Scout thinks Jem must have gotten up.
- The night is quiet again, except for the sound of a man wheezing.
- Scout calls out Jem's name, but he doesn't answer.
- Eventually Scout realizes that there's two men under the tree besides her and Jem.

- She says Atticus's name hesitatingly, but still gets no answer.
- The man walks towards the road, and Scout goes to where he had been, looking for Jem.
- Instead she finds a man lying on the ground smelling of booze.
- Scout finally makes her way over the road, and in the light of the street lamp Scout sees a man carrying Jem, whose arm is hanging at an unnatural angle.
- The man goes to the Finch house, where Atticus lets him in.
- Scout catches up and sees Aunt Alexandra running at her calling for the doctor, and hears her father in the next room asking where she is.
- Aunt Alexandra calls back to Atticus that Scout is there, and goes to the phone to call Doctor Reynolds.
- As she's hanging up Atticus comes into the room and calls the sheriff, telling him someone has attacked his kids and he should retrace their steps to see if he's still around.
- Aunt Alexandra de-hams Scout and asks her what happened, but Scout says she doesn't know.
- Dr. Reynolds arrives and tends to Jem first, who has a broken arm and a concussion, and then Scout, who's also gotten knocked around the head.
- Scout asks Dr. Reynolds if Jem is dead (more than once), but the doctor reassures her he'll be fine.
- After the doctor leaves Scout looks in on Jem, who's unconscious.
- Scout looks around Jem's room and sees Atticus, Aunt Alexandra, and a man she doesn't know; at that moment Mr. Tate arrives.
- They all sit down, except for the stranger.
- Mr. Tate says he's found a pink dress, some pieces of ham-colored cloth – and the corpse of Bob Ewell, who's been stabbed to death.

Chapter Twenty-Nine

- Aunt Alexandra and Atticus are shocked to hear that Mr. Ewell is dead.
- Aunt Alexandra leaves the room, and Mr. Tate asks Scout if she can tell them what happened.
- Scout climbs into Atticus's lap and tells the story: how she had forgotten her shoes, how they thought it was Cecil so they shouted at him (the sheriff interrupts here to ask if Atticus heard anything: he didn't, but he had the radio on); how she heard the footsteps behind them; how she was still wearing the ham costume.
- Mr. Tate says the costume explains the strange marks he found on the body, and Atticus goes to get the now squashed ham.
- They look at the costume, and it's more than squashed – there's a cut where Mr. Ewell had slashed at Scout with a knife.
- Atticus says he never thought Ewell would go after the kids, and Tate says that there are some men who are just bad.
- They go back to Scout's story: they were under the oak tree when something grabbed her, and then she heard fighting noises; Jem pulled her towards the road, then got pulled back; there was more fighting, and the sound of Jem's arm breaking, and his scream, and then silence; Scout went back to try to find Jem and nearly got suffocated by Mr. Ewell, when

the man was suddenly pulled away from her, she thinks by Jem.
- Scout continues: she heard a man wheezing and coughing, but it wasn't Jem, so she started feeling around for Jem on the ground.
- Tate asks who the other man was, and Scout gestures towards the stranger in the corner.
- Scout finally looks at the man properly and sees his paleness, his thinness, his colorless eyes, and realizes – she's looking at Boo Radley.
- He smiles shyly at her, and tears come to Scout's eyes as she says "Hey, Boo" (29.50).

Chapter Thirty

- Atticus reminds Scout she should call him Mr. Arthur, and formally introduces them to each other.
- Dr. Reynolds comes in and greets Boo, astonishing Scout with his nonchalance.
- They all go out to the front porch, leaving Dr. Reynolds to tend to Jem.
- Scout plays hostess to Boo, showing him the way and offering him a chair, though the whole thing feels not entirely real.
- Atticus starts talking about how he's going to make Jem's case in court, but Tate interrupts him to ask if he really thinks that Jem killed Ewell.
- Atticus says they'll have to talk to Jem to make sure, but from what Scout said it seems obvious.
- Tate says that Jem didn't do it, and Atticus says he appreciates the gesture, but he's not going to try to cover up the crime, because he doesn't roll like that.
- Tate says that there's not going to be a cover-up, and Scout thinks that there's a silent battle going on between them.
- Atticus asks Scout again who pulled Ewell off of her, and she says rather uncertainly that she thought it was Jem.
- Atticus interrupts Scout before she can go on to say that he wants everything to be aboveboard so that Jem won't have to live with any suspicion hanging over him.
- Tate says that Ewell fell on his knife and killed himself accidentally.
- Scout wonders whose stubbornness would win out – Tate's or her father's.
- Atticus says that he wouldn't be able to look Jem in the eye, and Jem wouldn't be able to look up to him, if he didn't act with absolute honor in this matter.
- Tate says again that Ewell stabbed himself, and adds that he can prove it.
- Atticus says that he simply can't be two-faced and say a thing he doesn't believe is true.
- Tate pulls out a knife (not the murder weapon) and demonstrates what he thinks happened (without the actual impaling, of course).
- Atticus continues in the same vein that he won't let Tate save Jem through lying, and Tate says (in italics, so we know he's getting mad) that it's not Jem he's trying to save, stamping his foot so loudly that both Miss Maudie's and Miss Stephanie's lights go on.
- Tate continues, more quietly, that no boy as small as Jem, with a broken arm no less, could take down an adult man in the dark.
- Atticus suddenly asks where Tate got that knife he was demonstrating with a second ago, and Tate says that he took it off a drunk, and that Ewell must have found the kitchen knife in the dump.

- Tate continues: it's his decision to make, and if Atticus goes around telling people that Jem killed Ewell, Tate will say that he's lying; Jem didn't stab him and Atticus knows it.
- Tate continues further: he's lived in Maycomb all his life, and knows everything that's happened there; Tom Robinson is dead, and now the man who all but killed him is dead too.
- He finishes: "let the dead bury the dead" (30.60).
- Oh wait, he's not quite done yet: he says that it's not a crime to prevent a crime, and that if he didn't keep quiet about what really happened all the Maycomb ladies come knocking on "his" (not Tate's, but he doesn't name names) door with their best cakes as thank-you gifts, and it would be a sin to call so much attention to a man who just wants to be left alone.
- Tate leaves, and Atticus says to Scout that Ewell killed himself accidentally, and asks her if she can understand.
- Scout hugs Atticus and tells him she does understand: it would be like killing a mockingbird.
- Atticus rubs Scout's hair, and the two of them head indoors.
- Before they go inside, Atticus turns to Boo Radley and thanks his neighbor for protecting his children.

Chapter Thirty-One

- Scout is surprised that the long-dreamed-of Boo Radley is actually next to her in the flesh.
- Boo nods towards the front door, and Atticus asks him to come in to say goodnight to Jem.
- They go into Jem's room, where Aunt Alexandra is sitting, and Scout leads Boo to Jem's bed.
- Boo looks at Jem with curiosity – "as though had never seen a boy before" (31.9), Scout thinks – and Scout encourages him to pet Jem's head while he's asleep and can't make a fuss about it.
- Scout, who's becoming sensitive to Boo's mute communications, realizes he wants to leave, so she leads him to the front porch.
- He asks her a in a quiet voice to take her home, and together they walk arm-in-arm to the Radley Place.
- As they walk Scout thinks of all the time they spent on this street thinking about Boo.
- Boo goes inside, and Scout never sees him again.
- Scout thinks about everything Boo had given them over the years, and is sad to realize that they had never given him anything in return.
- Scout turns to leave, and sees her neighborhood with fresh eyes from this spot where she's never stood before.
- She shifts slightly to stand in front of the shuttered window next to the front door, and imagines how the events of the past few years would have appeared to Boo from this window – how Boo would have looked on her, and Jem, and Atticus.
- Scout thinks about how Atticus always says you need to stand in a man's shoes before you can understand him, and how standing on the Radley porch helps her understand Boo.

- Scout walks home through the rain and thinks of how much she has to tell Jem, and how sore he's going to be that he was unconscious through the whole thing.
- Scout thinks that she and Jem may have some more growing to do, but there's not much left for them to learn, except maybe algebra.
- At home, Scout runs to Jem's room and finds Atticus there, reading.
- Atticus tells her that Jem won't be awake till morning and it's time for her to go to bed.
- Scout asks if she can sit up with him, and he lets her.
- Feeling sleepy already, Scout asks Atticus about his book, and he tells her that it's one of Jem's – *The Gray Ghost*.
- Scout asks him to read it out loud because it's nice and scary, but Atticus says that she's had enough scaring tonight.
- Scout says she wasn't scared – or at least not until she started telling the story of what happened – and that only books are really scary.
- Atticus starts reading aloud, and Scout falls asleep.
- Later Atticus puts Scout to bed, and a dozy Scout mutters that she heard every word of the story – about how they chased Stoner's Boy but they couldn't catch him because they'd never seen him, and when they found him he wasn't bad at all, but "real nice" (31.53)
- Atticus tells her: "Most people are, Scout, when you finally see them" (31.55).
- He goes back to Jem's room, where he will stay for the whole night, and "he would be there when Jem waked up in the morning" (31.56).

Themes

Theme of Race

To Kill a Mockingbird goes beyond the simple message "racism is bad" to attempt a more complex examination of how racism works. All forms of racism are not the same: some are born of hate, some of fear, some of laziness, some of self-righteousness, some of all these combined. What all racisms have in common in this book, however, is a failure of imagination: the inability to see that even someone who looks, and talks, and acts very different from oneself is fundamentally the same as every other human being. The history of race in the novel, as in America, is based on drawing distinctions solely for the sake of discrimination.

Questions About Race

1. How does the novel portray its African-American characters? Are there elements of racism in these portrayals?
2. How is the African-American community similar to the white community in Maycomb? How is it different? How might these similarities and differences affect how the two communities see each other?
3. How might Maycomb, and the events of the novel, be different if there were more than two races represented in the town?

Chew on Race

The African-American characters in *To Kill a Mockingbird* appear only to contribute to the development of the white characters, rather than as individuals in their own right.

To Kill a Mockingbird suggests that racism is learned, and therefore can be unlearned.

Theme of Justice and Judgment

To Kill a Mockingbird presents a judicial system that doesn't practice what it preaches. Ideally, a jury of one's peers dispassionately determines guilt or innocence based on the facts; but in practice, according to the novel, what actually happens is that a group of white men not influential enough to get out of jury duty give a verdict they had decided on before they even entered the courtroom. Is there any way for a justice system to overcome the unjust biases of the individuals who carry it out?

Questions About Justice and Judgment

1. Does Tom Robinson receive a fair trial under the law? Why are why not?
2. According to the novel, it is ever justified to act outside the law in order to ensure justice? If so, when is it justified? If not, what do you do when the law allows injustice?
3. What's the novel's take on the American legal system? What are its strengths, and what are its weakness?

Chew on Justice and Judgment

To Kill a Mockingbird suggests that the criminal court system is broken, but that it's still the best chance for justice.

To Kill a Mockingbird contrasts two kinds of justice – that of the courts and that of individuals – to show that they both have strengths and weaknesses.

Theme of Youth

Are kids just the mini-me versions of the adults they will become, or is something substantial lost – or gained – in the transition to adulthood? And how does that process work, anyhow? *To Kill a Mockingbird* shows a child's perspective on adult events, and suggests that while children aren't just adults in miniature, they also aren't what adults imagine or misremember children to be. The novel suggests that adulthood is both a gain and a loss – and some of the abilities that disappear – like fairness, compassion, and a critical way of looking at the world – are well worth trying to keep.

Questions About Youth

1. How does the novel portray children as different from adults?
2. What difference does it make to the novel that it's narrated from a child's perspective? How would the book be different if an adult perspective was dominant?

3. According to the novel, what happens in the process of growing up? What factors determine what kind of adult a child becomes?
4. Is identity fixed in childhood, or can it change over time?

Chew on Youth

The children in the novel reveal what the adults can't see, through their innocent perspective on events.

The novel's association of children with fairness suggests that a sense of justice is innate, not learned, and therefore adults must have learned to be unjust.

Theme of Morality and Ethics

Are morals a matter of community standards or individual conscience? Where do the rights of the community end and the rights of the individual begin? *To Kill a Mockingbird* examines the conflict between the individual and the community when each has a different standard of right and wrong. On the one hand, the individual who stands up for his or her personal belief gets grief from everyone else. But on the other, such solitary stubbornness might drag the whole community in a more satisfactory direction – a community's morals are, after all, the sum of what its individuals believe.

Questions About Morality and Ethics

1. What do individual characters in the novel base their ideas of right and wrong on?
2. How does the community work to enforce collective standards of morality? Where do those collective standards come from?
3. What moral principles does the novel suggest are desirable? Does anything in the novel undermine these moral principles?
4. Does Bob Ewell have bad morals or no morals? What's the difference?

Chew on Morality and Ethics

Atticus presents himself as morally consistent – the same at home as on the streets – but really he has two moral systems: one for himself based on strict rectitude, and one for others based on sympathetic understanding.

While the novel in general presents honesty as a virtue, it also suggests that honesty is not always the best policy.

Theme of Fear

Early in *To Kill a Mockingbird*, the novel paraphrases Franklin D. Roosevelt's inaugural address: "the only thing we have to fear is fear itself." But fear, itself, can be very scary when it hijacks people's reason and compassion for others. As another great statesman, Yoda, put it,

"Fear leads to anger. Anger leads to hate. Hate leads to suffering." And where does that all leave us? The Dark Side, or in this case, racism, injustice, harassment, and senseless killing. Fear makes people lash out against what scares them in order to restore their comfort zone, even if they have to destroy innocent lives along the way.

Questions About Fear

1. Tom is disabled and seems like a nice, unthreatening guy. Why might Maycomb be so scared of him?
2. Why is Mayella so frightened on the witness stand?
3. What does the novel say about what things should be considered scary, and what shouldn't?
4. How do fear and race relate to each other in the novel?

Chew on Fear

A specific fear fuels Maycomb's desire to convict Tom: the fear that if Mayella's accusation is revealed as false, other African-American men will commit the crime of which Tom is falsely accused.

A significant part of growing up for Scout is losing her fear of the unknown.

Theme of Women and Femininity

Being called a girl is about the worst thing possible – or so thinks Scout, the female protagonist of *To Kill a Mockingbird*. Girls wear frilly pink dresses, and don't get to play outside, swear, or pretty much do anything fun. Even less appealing to the tomboy Scout, at least at first, is the thought of growing up into a lady, and being plunged into a confusing world where no one says what they mean. As the novel progresses, however, so do Scout's views on femininity, as she realizes that being a lady requires skill, and sometimes even courage.

Questions About Women and Femininity

1. Why does Scout take being called a girl as an insult?
2. What effect does their lack of a mother have on Jem and Scout?
3. What models of femininity do the different female characters in the novel demonstrate for Scout?

Chew on Women and Femininity

To Kill a Mockingbird suggests that questioning the "polite fiction" of "Southern womanhood" (15.39) has the potential to undermine not just gender attitudes, but racial ones as well.

Scout's reluctance to be feminine both asserts and denies her maturity, and is a way for her to try to grow up on her own terms.

Theme of Family

In *To Kill a Mockingbird*, family is destiny. Within the confines of a small town where the same people have lived for generations, no one can escape...becoming their parents. Either the parents raise their kids to be like them, for good or ill, or the pressure of community expectations that a person live up, or down, to their family is too much to resist. While on the one hand, this attitude creates a comfortable familiarity and a cozy predictability, it also makes progress, both for the individual and the community, very difficult.

Questions About Family

1. What's the effect of having the Finch children call their father by his first name? What does that suggest about their characters? About his? Their relationship?
2. Why is Aunt Alexandra so obsessed with Old Family and Finch pride? What does she hope to accomplish by making Scout and Jem feel that as well?
3. How does family intersect with class in the novel?
4. What do the examples of good and bad parents in the novel suggest about the best way to raise kids?
5. How does Maycomb's African-American community think about the idea of family?

Chew on Family

To Kill a Mockingbird suggests that depending on the family a person is born into, s/he may be doomed from the start: personal merit can't overcome a poor inheritance.

The way family is used in the novel suggests that characters find it easier to think about people as groups rather than as individuals.

Theme of Compassion and Forgiveness

How do you manage compassion for people when they are undeserving? This is a central question in *To Kill a Mockingbird*. The answer? A little goodness, a little humility, and a lot of imagination. While from the outside a person may seem vile, stupid, or just plain incomprehensible, imagining what it's like inside that person's head can do wonders for understanding them. Of course, there's also the danger that you'll be wrong about just how nasty that person really is, but that's the risk of being a good person.

Questions About Compassion and Forgiveness

1. Is there anyone who the novel suggests isn't deserving of compassion and forgiveness? Who, and why?
2. What does whom a character feels sorry for reveal about that character?
3. Is compassion learned or innate in the novel? Or both?
4. Why does Atticus refuse to pity Mayella?

Chew on Compassion and Forgiveness

By having Atticus be a figure associated both with justice and with compassion, the novel suggests that the two ideas are not mutually exclusive.

Tom's compassion for Mayella and Atticus's compassion for Ewell both get them into trouble, suggesting compassion can sometimes be dangerous.

Quotes

Race Quotes

"Scout," said Atticus, "nigger-lover is just one of those terms that don't mean anything – like snot-nose. It's hard to explain – ignorant, trashy people use it when they think somebody's favoring Negroes over and above themselves. It's slipped into usage with some people like ourselves, when they want a common, ugly term to label somebody."

"You aren't really a nigger-lover, then, are you?"

"I certainly am. I do my best to love everybody... I'm hard put, sometimes – baby, it's never an insult to be called what somebody thinks is a bad name. It just shows you how poor that person is, it doesn't hurt you." (11.107-109)

Thought: In giving Scout a lesson in How Racism Works 101, Atticus also does the same for the audience. On the syllabus in this conversation: the power of language, not only as a way to shame those who don't toe the racist line, but also to set the terms of the debate. Racists use "nigger-lover" to suggest that a person is trying to give African-Americans special rights, but Atticus points out that all he's arguing for is equality, loving everybody the same. The end of the quote is basically a grown-up version of "I'm rubber and you're glue," suggesting that schoolyard taunt actually has some merit – some insults do tell you more about the person hurling them than about their target.

Lula stopped, but she said, "You ain't got no business bringin' white chillun here – they got their church, we got our'n. It is our church, ain't it, Miss Cal?"

Calpurnia said, "It's the same God, ain't it?"

Jem said, "Let's go home, Cal, they don't want us here-"

I agreed: they did not want us here. I sensed, rather than saw, that we were being advanced upon. They seemed to be drawing closer to us, but when I looked up at Calpurnia there was amusement in her eyes. When I looked down the pathway again, Lula was gone. In her place was a solid mass of colored people.

One of them stepped from the crowd. It was Zeebo, the garbage collector. "Mister Jem," he said, "we're mighty glad to have you all here. Don't pay no 'tention to Lula, she's contentious because Reverend Sykes threatened to church her. She's a troublemaker from way back, got fancy ideas an' haughty ways – we're mighty glad to have you all." (12.48-52)

Thought: One criticism leveled against this novel is that all the African-American characters are docile lambs, humbly grateful whenever the white characters bother to treat them like the human beings they are. Lula is the one exception, the lone angry voice suggesting that the Finch children's appearance at the First Purchase Church is an invasion rather than a blessing. While she's swiftly silenced, her brief flare-up suggests a more critical perspective of the "good" white people in the novel, as well as of the other African-American characters who are so quick to play down her objections.

That Calpurnia led a modest double life never dawned on me. The idea that she had a separate existence outside our household was a novel one, to say nothing of her having command of two languages.

"Cal," I asked, "why do you talk nigger-talk to the – to your folks when you know it's not right?"

"Well, in the first place I'm black-"

"That doesn't mean you hafta talk that way when you know better," said Jem. [...]

"It's right hard to say," she said. "Suppose you and Scout talked colored-folks' talk at home it'd be out of place, wouldn't it? Now what if I talked white-folks' talk at church, and with my neighbors? They'd think I was puttin' on airs to beat Moses."

"But Cal, you know better," I said.

"It's not necessary to tell all you know. It's not ladylike – in the second place, folks don't like to have somebody around knowin' more than they do. It aggravates 'em. You're not gonna change any of them by talkin' right, they've got to want to learn themselves, and when they don't want to learn there's nothing you can do but keep your mouth shut or talk their language." (12.138-144)

Thought: Calpurnia's words here sound kind of like Atticus's repeated statement that he wants to be the same person at home as he is in the streets. Scout and Jem at first think that Calpurnia should do the same, but her explanation of her "double life" is that sometimes conformity to what everyone else is doing makes more sense. Calpurnia and Atticus offer different models to Jem and Scout of how to deal with a world that often can't deal with who people really are. (Extra credit: Check out W.E.B. DuBois's "Of Our Spiritual Strivings" in the "Links" section for a famous discussion of doubleness and African-American identity.)

"Well how do you know we ain't Negroes?"

"Uncle Jack Finch says we really don't know. He says as far as he can trace back the Finches we ain't, but for all he knows we mighta come straight out of Ethiopia durin' the Old Testament."

"Well if we came out durin' the Old Testament it's too long ago to matter."

"That's what I thought," said Jem, "but around here once you have a drop of Negro blood, that makes you all black." (16.78-81)

Thought: Jem and Scout here try to figure out how society divides people up into races, and what happens when those divisions break down. As kids who don't yet simply accept the existing system as the Way Things Are Just Because, they are able to see that the "one-drop rule" doesn't really work unless the origin of every drop of a person's blood (or every gene in their DNA, to update their science) can be accounted for, and why is one drop of black blood able to overwhelm several gallons of white blood, anyway? And how can blood have a racial identity? By having Jem and Scout puzzle over these questions without coming up with any answers, the novel suggests that the reason they can't crack the puzzle is that there is no solution – the "common knowledge" simply doesn't make sense.

[Mr. Ewell says] "I seen that black nigger yonder ruttin' on my Mayella!" [...]

As Judge Taylor banged his gavel, Mr. Ewell was sitting smugly in the witness chair, surveying his handiwork. With one phrase he had turned happy picknickers into a sulky, tense, murmuring crowd, being slowly hypnotized by gavel taps lessening in intensity until the only sound in the courtroom was a dim pink-pink-pink: the judge might have been rapping the bench with a pencil. (17.84, 95)

Thought: Mr. Ewell may be barely literate, but he's a veritable Shakespeare when it comes to offensive language. The way he phrases his accusation achieves an impressive feat of multitasking: it 1) dehumanizes Tom (he doesn't use Tom's name, or even the pronoun "he"), 2) emphasizes Tom's race over everything else (the redundancy of "black nigger"), 3) compares Tom to a beast ("rutting" is usually applied to animals), 4) portrays Mayella as a passive victim (she's the indirect object of the sentence), and 5) asserts power over his daughter ("my Mayella," as if Tom's trying to steal Ewell's property). Not bad for a mere ten words – no wonder the crowd goes wild.

[Atticus says] "What was the evidence of her offense? Tom Robinson, a human being. She must put Tom Robinson away from her. Tom Robinson was her daily reminder of what she did. What did she do? She tempted a Negro.

"She was white, and she tempted a Negro. She did something that in our society is unspeakable: she kissed a black man. Not an old Uncle, but a strong young Negro man. No code mattered to her before she broke it, but it came crashing down on her afterwards."

(20.44-45)

Thought: This passage suggests a question: why do the citizens of Maycomb (or at least some of them) prefer to believe that a black man raped a white woman than that a white woman kissed a black man? The word "tempted" seems kind of strange here, considering Tom's reaction to her advances seemed less "I totally would, but they'd totally kill me" than "just not that into you, kthxbye." "Tempted" does suggest that Mayella's not only being a "bad" white person here, but also a "bad" woman in being sexual at all, let alone choosing a forbidden object of desire. For her to desire a black man goes against the accepted order of things in both race (white is desirable, black is not) and gender (men desire, women are desired), which is just too crazy, not to mention dangerous to the status quo, for people to deal with.

[Atticus says] "The witnesses for the state, with the exception of the sheriff of Maycomb County, have presented themselves to you gentlemen, to this court, in the cynical confidence that their testimony would not be doubted, confident that you gentlemen would go along with them on the assumption – the evil assumption – that all Negroes lie, that all Negroes are basically immoral beings, that all Negro men are not to be trusted around our women, an assumption one associates with minds of their caliber.

"Which, gentlemen, we know is in itself a lie as black as Tom Robinson's skin, a lie I do not have to point out to you. You know the truth, and the truth is this: some Negroes lie, some Negroes are immoral, some Negro men are not to be trusted around women – black or white. But this is a truth that applies to the human race and to no particular race of men. There is not a person in this courtroom who has never told a lie, who has never done an immoral thing, and there is no man living who has never looked upon a woman without desire." (20.47-48)

Thought: In his closing remarks, Atticus appeals to a common humanity over divisive racial stereotypes, and calls out the prosecution for arguing that Tom's blackness is itself evidence of his guilt. Arguing that crime isn't limited to one race, that black men aren't the only ones who lie or rape or shoplift or deal drugs, at first seems like a poor rhetorical choice in this context: saying "some black men are rapists...but this one isn't!" doesn't seem to be the most effective closing statement in the rape trial of a black man. Perhaps Atticus is doing what he did when he earlier talked about the case to Uncle Jack, knowing that Scout was listening outside the door: speaking to the larger audience as much as, or more than the jury, about attitudes towards race that extend beyond this particular case. There's also a bit of irony here, in that Atticus calls the lie of racist stereotypes "as black as Tom Robinson's skin," once again associating evilness with blackness, although in a more figurative way.

"If you had been on that jury, son, and eleven other boys like you, Tom would be a free man," said Atticus. "So far nothing in your life has interfered with your reasoning process. Those are twelve reasonable men in everyday life, Tom's jury, but you saw something come between them and reason. [...] There's something in our world that makes men lose their heads – they couldn't be fair if they tried. In our courts, when it's a white man's word against a black man's, the white man always wins. They're ugly, but those are the facts of life. [...]

"The one place where a man ought to get a square deal is in a courtroom, be he any color of the rainbow, but people have a way of carrying their resentments right into a jury box." (23.38-40)

Thought: According to Atticus here, there's just something about race that makes white people crazy. His holding up Jem as an exception because of his youth suggests that whatever that X factor is, it's learned and not innate (and thus, perhaps can be changed through education?). He also acknowledges, in case it wasn't already obvious, that law isn't a pure realm free of the prejudices that plague everyday life – it's subject to the same problems as society at large. Usually Atticus is a voice of hope for change, but here he flatly says that racism is a "fact of life," suggesting that losing Tom's case severely dented his optimism concerning human nature – or else that, having sat through the case, Jem is ready to hear a truer, grimmer version of how the world works, instead of the sanitized Disney version.

[Atticus says] "As you grow older, you'll see white men cheat black men every day of your life, but let me tell you something and don't you forget it – whenever a white man does that to a black man, no matter who he is, how rich he is, or how fine a family he comes from, that white man is trash." Atticus was speaking so quietly his last word crashed on our ears. I looked up, and his face was vehement. "There's nothing more sickening to me than a low-grade white man who'll take advantage of a Negro's ignorance. Don't fool yourselves – it's all adding up and one of these days we're going to pay the bill for it. I hope it's not in you children's time." (23.40)

Thought: Atticus's words suggest that moral choices don't take place in a vacuum – in an unequal system, cheating someone who's already systemically screwed over is even worse than just plain old cheating. This statement is made all the more powerful by Atticus's general mild-manneredness and refusal to, well, trash people throughout the novel, showing just how important this principle is to him, or at least how much he wants to impress it on his kids. (And the last line of the quote is a reminder that the book was written not in the 1930s, when it takes place, but in the late 1950s, as the civil rights struggle was just beginning to heat up.)

To Maycomb, Tom's death was typical. Typical of a nigger to cut and run. Typical of a nigger's mentality to have no plan, no thought for the future, just run blind first chance he saw. Funny thing, Atticus Finch might've got him off scot free, but wait-? Hell no. You know how they are. Easy come, easy go. Just shows you, that Robinson boy was legally married, they say he kept himself clean, went to church and all that, but when it comes down to the line the veneer's mighty thin. Nigger always comes out in 'em. (25.25)

Thought: For all the talk of baby steps and the folks with background who oppose racism from Atticus and Miss Maudie, this passage suggests that not much has changed in Maycomb after Tom's trial, and there's still a long way to go.

Justice and Judgment Quotes

"Atticus, you must be wrong...."

"How's that?"

"Well, most folks seem to think they're right and you're wrong...."

"They're certainly entitled to think that, and they're entitled to full respect for their opinions," said Atticus, "but before I can live with other folks I've got to live with myself. The one thing that doesn't abide by majority rule is a person's conscience." (11.54-57)

Thought: Majority rule doesn't determine individual standards of right and wrong, but what about community standards? Isn't that what a jury does, vote on what is just in a particular case?

"You goin' to court this morning?" asked Jem. [...]

"I am not. 't's morbid, watching a poor devil on trial for his life. Look at all those folks, it's like a Roman carnival."

"They hafta try him in public, Miss Maudie," I said. "Wouldn't be right if they didn't."

"I'm quite aware of that," she said. "Just because it's public, I don't have to go, do I?" (16.40-48)

Thought: While Tom's trial is on the one hand a major moment for (the denial of) civil rights in Maycomb, it's also perceived as entertainment. Miss Maudie's refusal to attend is also a refusal to join the group of people who see the trial as a fun day out.

So far, things were utterly dull: nobody had thundered, there were no arguments between opposing counsel, there was no drama; a grave disappointment to all present, it seemed. Atticus was proceeding amiably, as if he were involved in a title dispute. With his infinite capacity for calming turbulent seas, he could make a rape case as dry as a sermon. (17.56)

Thought: The battle between prosecution and defense is also a battle between emotion and reason. Atticus's calm, rational demeanor provides a model for how he hopes the jury will behave.

As Judge Taylor banged his gavel, Mr. Ewell was sitting smugly in the witness chair, surveying his handiwork. With one phrase he had turned happy picknickers into a sulky, tense, murmuring crowd, being slowly hypnotized by gavel taps lessening in intensity until the only sound in the courtroom was a dim pink-pink-pink: the judge might have been rapping the bench with a pencil. (17.95)

Thought: While Atticus tries to keep the case in the realm of legal logic, Ewell blatantly appeals to hate and fear. His effect on the crows suggests that his approach rings a very loud bell with them, though Judge Taylor's ability to calm them down implies that they might be open to the other side's persuasion as well.

"It was just him I couldn't stand," Dill said. [...] "That old Mr. Gilmer doin' him thataway, talking so hateful to him – [...] It was the way he said it made me sick, plain sick. [...] The way that man called him 'boy' all the time an' sneered at him, an' looked around at the jury every time he answered-[...] It ain't right, somehow it ain't right to do 'em that way. Hasn't anybody got any business talkin' like that – it just makes me sick." (19.155-165)

Thought: Dill picks up on the subtle cues Mr. Gilmer uses to influence the jury against Tom, and recognizes that they aren't fair play. He sees that the emperor has no clothes – that Mr. Gilmer isn't acting that way because Tom *is* inferior, but because he wants to remind the jury every second to *think* Tom is inferior and a likely criminal.

"She has committed no crime, she has merely broken a rigid and time-honored code of our society, a code so severe that whoever breaks it is hounded from our midst as unfit to live with. She is the victim of cruel poverty and ignorance, but I cannot pity her: she is white. She knew full well the enormity of her offense, but because her desires were stronger than the code she was breaking, she persisted in breaking it. [...]

"What did she do? She tempted a Negro.

"She was white, and she tempted a Negro. She did something that in our society is unspeakable: she kissed a black man. Not an old Uncle, but a strong young Negro man. No code mattered to her before she broke it, but it came crashing down on her afterwards." (20.43-45)

Thought: Atticus is implying here that the real violation here is Mayella's breaking of the code that says she can't do anything sexual with an African-American man. Accusing Tom of rape is the closest the law can get to dealing with this transgression of society's unwritten code. But is Mayella really to blame? Being attracted to Tom is not in itself wrong, though her society thinks it is, but perhaps what is wrong is acting selfishly without any concern for the situation she was putting Tom in, and the consequences it would have for him.

"But there is one way in this country in which all men are created equal – there is one human institution that makes a pauper the equal of a Rockefeller, the stupid man the equal of an Einstein, and the ignorant man the equal of any college president. That institution, gentlemen, is a court. [...] Our courts have their faults, as does any human institution, but in this country our courts are the great levelers, and in our courts all men are created equal.

"I'm no idealist to believe firmly in the integrity of our courts and in the jury system – that is no ideal to me, it is a living, working reality. Gentlemen, a court is no better than each man of you

sitting before me on this jury. A court is only as sound as its jury, and a jury is only as sound as the men who make it up. I am confident that you gentlemen will review without passion the evidence you have heard, come to a decision, and restore this defendant to his family. In the name of God, do your duty." (20.51-52)

Thought: While Atticus says that he's no idealist here, the fact that he's been realistic throughout about his extremely low chances of winning this case suggests that Atticus has a "be the change you wish to see in the world" bumper sticker on his car: he's acting as if the outcome he knows is impossible is actually the only possible income, in an attempt to make it so.

Atticus was saying, "With people like us – that's our share of the bill. We generally get the juries we deserve. Our stout Maycomb citizens aren't interested, in the first place. In the second place, they're afraid. [..] Well, what if – say, Mr. Link Deas had to decide the amount of damages to award, say, Miss Maudie, when Miss Rachel ran over her with a car. Link wouldn't like the thought of losing either lady's business at his store, would he? So he tells Judge Taylor that he can't serve on the jury because he doesn't have anybody to keep store for him while he's gone. So Judge Taylor excuses him. Sometimes he excuses him wrathfully." (23.46-49)

Thought: Personal concerns trump public duty before the jury even hears the case. The idea of "a jury of one's peers," already suspect when only white men are allowed to serve on juries, becomes even more problematic when one's peers avoid serving at all costs. And who would Tom Robinson's "peers" for the purposes of jury selection be?

How could this be so, I wondered, as I read Mr. Underwood's editorial. Senseless killing – Tom had been given due process of law to the day of his death; he had been tried openly and convicted by twelve good men and true; my father had fought for him all the way. Then Mr. Underwood's meaning became clear: Atticus had used every tool available to free men to save Tom Robinson, but in the secret courts of men's hearts Atticus had no case. Tom was a dead man the minute Mayella Ewell opened her mouth and screamed. (25.28)

Thought: Just as the real transgression is Mayella's breaking of the code of segregation, the real trial takes place in the "secret courts of men hearts." Is the public trial then pointless? What, if anything, did it accomplish?

"I'm not a very good man, sir, but I am sheriff of Maycomb County. Lived in this town all my life an' I'm goin' on forty-three years old. Know everything that's happened here since before I was born. There's a black boy dead for no reason, and the man responsible for it's dead. Let the dead bury the dead this time, Mr. Finch. Let the dead bury the dead." (30.60)

Thought: In Heck Tate's eyes, justice has been carried out in the death of Ewell, and looking too closely at how that came about does no one any good.

Youth Quotes

Atticus had promised me he would wear me out if he ever heard of me fighting any more; I was far too old and too big for such childish things, and the sooner I learned to hold in, the better off everybody would be. (9.1)

Thought: Growing up is also growing in, and putting up walls of self-control so that others can't see what's inside. While on the one hand once Scout figures out how to do this she'll get in less trouble, on the other this is a kind of hypocrisy.

"When a child asks you something, answer him, for goodness' sake. But don't make a production of it. Children are children, but they can spot an evasion quicker than adults, and evasion simply muddles 'em." (9.175)

Thought: While Atticus respects his children, he also recognizes that they're different from adults. Still, for Atticus treating them as children doesn't mean lying to them or avoiding hard truths (does this mean no Santa Claus for the Finch kids?).

When we were small, Jem and I confined our activities to the southern neighborhood, but when I was well into the second grade at school and tormenting Boo Radley became passe, the business section of Maycomb drew us frequently up the street past the real property of Mrs. Henry Lafayette Dubose. It was impossible to go to town without passing her house unless we wished to walk a mile out of the way. Previous minor encounters with her left me with no desire for more, but Jem said I had to grow up some time. (11.1)

Thought: Another aspect of growing up: having to face unpleasant things instead of avoiding them. While it would seem that growing up would give a person more power, it also makes it less likely that s/he is able to do what s/he wants (at least for some things).

Dill's eyes flickered at Jem, and Jem looked at the floor. Then he rose and broke the remaining code of our childhood. He went out of the room and down the hall. "Atticus," his voice was distant, "can you come here a minute, sir?"

Beneath its sweat-streaked dirt Dill's face went white. I felt sick. [...]

Jem was standing in a corner of the room, looking like the traitor he was. "Dill, I had to tell him," he said. "You can't run three hundred miles off without your mother knowin'."

We left him without a word. (14.79-91)

Thought: Jem really is growing up – he puts adult notions of what's right (tell your parents before you decide to run off to a different county) before child ones (don't tattle on your friends). Is there a particular reason for Jem's change, or is it just part of getting older?

I raised up on my elbow, facing Dill's outline. "It's no reason to run off. They don't get around to doin' what they say they're gonna do half the time...." (14.109)

Thought: While kids get a bum rap for having short attention spans, it's adults who can't be trusted to follow through from the child perspective. But has Scout shared anything from her own experience that supports this view, or is she just sympathizing with Dill?

"There has been a request," Judge Taylor said, "that this courtroom be cleared of spectators, or at least of women and children, a request that will be denied for the time being. People generally see what they look for, and hear what they listen for, and they have the right to subject their children to it, but I can assure you of one thing: you will receive what you see and hear in silence or you will leave this courtroom, but you won't leave it until the whole boiling of you come before me on contempt charges. (17.97)

Thought: Women are here put in the same category with children as beings in need of protection, whose delicate ears should be shielded from sordid reality. Never mind that rape is something women have to worry about experiencing more than men – they still shouldn't be allowed to hear about it.

But why had he entrusted us with his deepest secret? I asked him why.

"Because you're children and you can understand it," he said, "and because I heard that one-"

He jerked his head at Dill: "Things haven't caught up with that one's instinct yet. Let him get a little older and he won't get sick and cry. Maybe things'll strike him as being – not quite right, say, but he won't cry, not when he gets a few years on him."

"Cry about what, Mr. Raymond?" Dill's maleness was beginning to assert itself.

"Cry about the simple hell people give other people – without even thinking. Cry about the hell white people give colored folks, without even stopping to think that they're people, too." (20.18-22)

Thought: While kids haven't shut the display of emotions down yet, they also haven't dammed up their intake of impressions from the outside. Calling it "instinct" implies that this way of relating to the world is something everyone naturally has – is it possible to get back to this way of thinking (or not thinking), or is it a kind of innocence that is lost forever with growing up?

"Atticus-" said Jem bleakly.

He turned in the doorway. "What, son?"

"How could they do it, how could they?"

"I don't know, but they did it. They've done it before and they did it tonight and they'll do it again and when they do it – seems that only children weep. Good night." (22.14-17)

Thought: Is it "children" who are weeping, or only Jem, Scout, and Dill? Is it simply being children that causes them to be sad about Tom's fate, or are their other factors? If there are other factors, are they something only children can have, or can adults share them too? Mr. Raymond seems more upset than most of the adults about Tom's fate – what does he have in common with the Finch kids?

"Don't talk like that, Dill," said Aunt Alexandra. "It's not becoming to a child. It's – cynical."

"I ain't cynical, Miss Alexandra. Tellin' the truth's not cynical, is it?"

"The way you tell it, it is." (22.32-34)

Thought: Aunt Alexandra has an idea of what childlike behavior is – sweet and innocent, the Olsen twins before they hit puberty – and expects Dill to conform to that. This suggests that the idea of childhood isn't entirely natural – it's also what adults expect children to be like.

The adults in Maycomb never discussed the case with Jem and me; it seemed that they discussed it with their children, and their attitude must have been that neither of us could help having Atticus for a parent, so their children must be nice to us in spite of him. The children would never have thought that up for themselves: had our classmates been left to their own devices, Jem and I would have had several swift, satisfying fist-fights apiece and ended the matter for good. As it was, we were compelled to hold our heads high and be, respectively, a gentleman and a lady. (26.10)

Thought: Faced with a conflict caused by a dust-up in the adult world, the children are forced to act like adults. While the adult approach is less violent, bottling up those emotions means that they fester more than they would otherwise. Would matters have calmed down faster in Maycomb if, instead of a trial, there had been a celebrity death match between the two sides?

Morality and Ethics Quotes

"There's some folks who don't eat like us," she whispered fiercely, "but you ain't called on to contradict 'em at the table when they don't. That boy's yo' comp'ny and if he wants to eat up the table cloth you let him, you hear?"

"He ain't company, Cal, he's just a Cunningham-"

"Hush your mouth! Don't matter who they are, anybody sets foot in this house's yo' comp'ny, and don't you let me catch you remarkin' on their ways like you was so high and mighty! Yo' folks might be better'n the Cunninghams but it don't count for nothin' the way you're disgracin' 'em – if you can't act fit to eat at the table you can just set here and eat in the

kitchen!"

Calpurnia sent me through the swinging door to the diningroom with a stinging smack. (3.26-29)

Thought: Cal's moral lesson here is to respect people's differences, even if you think you're better than them. And acting like you're better than other people is the surest way to show that you're not. This interaction is an early blow against the stereotype that white people have morals but African-Americans don't.

"There are just some kind of men who – who're so busy worrying about the next world they've never learned to live in this one, and you can look down the street and see the results." (5.44)

Thought: Miss Maudie's talking about Nathan Radley here, but also about his fellow foot-washing Baptists who think she's going to hell for making her garden pretty. Not a party girl herself, Miss Maudie still strikes out at those who think that all pleasure is bad, except for the pleasure they obviously take in judging their neighbors as sinners.

"If you shouldn't be defendin' him, then why are you doin' it?"

"For a number of reasons," said Atticus. "The main one is, if I didn't I couldn't hold up my head in town, I couldn't represent this county in the legislature, I couldn't even tell you or Jem not to do something again." [...]

"Atticus, are we going to win it?"

"No, honey."

"Then why-"

"Simply because we were licked a hundred years before we started is no reason for us not to try to win," Atticus said. (9.16-25)

Thought: For Atticus, his own self-respect is bound up with his good morals – if he did something he knew was wrong, even if it was justified, he would lose all moral authority over others. It's interesting that the judgment he faces is solely his own – he's not worried about other people's criticism, or that they would vote him out of the legislature, or that Scout and Jem wouldn't respect him – he just wouldn't feel able to do any of those things if he didn't do right by Tom Robinson.

"Son, I have no doubt that you've been annoyed by your contemporaries about me lawing for niggers, as you say, but to do something like this to a sick old lady is inexcusable. I strongly advise you to go down and have a talk with Mrs. Dubose," said Atticus. "Come straight home afterward." (11.43)

Thought: Even when others do things that Atticus would rather eat spiders than do, he still thinks they should be treated with respect. In his moral system, just because Mrs. Dubose strikes out at Jem doesn't mean he's allowed to strike back. Atticus is definitely a New Testament kind of guy, turning the other cheek rather than going after an eye for an eye.

"Atticus, you must be wrong...."

"How's that?"

"Well, most folks seem to think they're right and you're wrong...."

"They're certainly entitled to think that, and they're entitled to full respect for their opinions," said Atticus, "but before I can live with other folks I've got to live with myself. The one thing that doesn't abide by majority rule is a person's conscience." (11.54-57)

Thought: Here Atticus is talking about how to balance the rights of the individual with the rights of the community. While democracy determines how the group will act, it can't control what a person thinks: the jury can vote to find Tom guilty, but it can't make everyone in Maycomb believe that he is so.

I said I would like it very much, which was a lie, but one must lie under certain circumstances and at all times when one can't do anything about them. (13.20)

Thought: This suggests that Scout has already learned the lessons of Cal's two languages and Mr. Raymond's phony drinking : that sometimes doing what people want you to do is the best way.

"Link, that boy might go to the chair, but he's not going till the truth's told." Atticus's voice was even. "And you know what the truth is." (15.23)

Thought: Atticus knows it's more unlikely than a Paris Hilton presidency that Tom will be acquitted, and yet getting the truth out there is still an accomplishment – although it's not obvious here, or perhaps ever, what it will accomplish.

"You know the truth, and the truth is this: some Negroes lie, some Negroes are immoral, some Negro men are not to be trusted around women – black or white. But this is a truth that applies to the human race and to no particular race of men. There is not a person in this courtroom who has never told a lie, who has never done an immoral thing, and there is no man living who has never looked upon a woman without desire." (20.48)

Thought: Atticus here points out the faulty moral logic of racism that goes Tom is black, black is bad, therefore Tom is bad, and tries to transform it into Tom is a man, some men are bad, some men are good, look at Tom and decide which group he falls into. Convicting Tom because he is black, Atticus argues, would be a silly as convicting him because he is a human being.

"Heck," Atticus's back was turned. "If this thing's hushed up it'll be a simple denial to Jem of the way I've tried to raise him. Sometimes I think I'm a total failure as a parent, but I'm all they've got. Before Jem looks at anyone else he looks at me, and I've tried to live so I can look squarely back at him... if I connived at something like this, frankly I couldn't meet his eye, and the day I can't do that I'll know I've lost him. I don't want to lose him and Scout, because they're all I've got." (30.37)

Thought: Atticus often says that he does the right thing because of his kids – that he wouldn't be able to ask for their respect if he didn't. Perhaps part of it is the desire to be a good example, but here it also seems that it's a matter of avoiding hypocrisy, of not wanting to ask Jem to be a better person than Atticus himself has managed to be. Or perhaps that's just the way Atticus gives his moral power a boost when he's feeling weak, or an easy way for Atticus to justify his own difficult moral choices to others.

"I never heard tell that it's against the law for a citizen to do his utmost to prevent a crime from being committed, which is exactly what he did, but maybe you'll say it's my duty to tell the town all about it and not hush it up. Know what'd happen then? All the ladies in Maycomb includin' my wife'd be knocking on his door bringing angel food cakes. To my way of thinkin', Mr. Finch, taking the one man who's done you and this town a great service an' draggin' him with his shy ways into the limelight – to me, that's a sin. It's a sin and I'm not about to have it on my head. If it was any other man, it'd be different. But not this man, Mr. Finch." (30.62)

Thought: The law is silent, or at least only whispers quietly, about this situation, so the conflict is on a moral level rather than a legal one. Atticus thinks about the right of the community to know, while Tate is more concerned about Boo's right to privacy. In the end, Atticus gives in to Tate's argument that Boo's individual rights trump the interest of the community – and it probably doesn't hurt that the community would mostly approve of what Boo did anyway.

Fear Quotes

But Dill got him the third day, when he told Jem that folks in Meridian certainly weren't as afraid as the folks in Maycomb, that he'd never seen such scary folks as the ones in Maycomb. [...]

Jem wanted Dill to know once and for all that he wasn't scared of anything: "It's just that I can't think of a way to make him come out without him gettin' us." Besides, Jem had his little sister to think of.

When he said that, I knew he was afraid. (1.71-75)

Thought: For Jem fear, however well-founded, is a source of shame. This might suggest another reason for the kids' obsession with Boo: acting like they're not scared of him is a way for them to show off to each other.

As the summer progressed, so did our game. We polished and perfected it, added dialogue and plot until we had manufactured a small play upon which we rang changes every day. (4.95)

Thought: Play-acting Boo's life might be a way for the kids to deal with their fear; maybe making it a game makes it easier for them to forget about its basis in reality.

Jem said quietly, "My sister ain't dirty and I ain't scared of you," although I noticed his knees shaking. (11.78)

Thought: Despite being a frail old lady in a wheelchair, Mrs. Dubose's tongue-lashings are enough to produce fear. Sticks and stones may break your bones, but words can make you go medieval on a camellia bush and get detention for a month.

Gone was the terror in my mind of stale whiskey and barnyard smells, of sleepy-eyed sullen men, of a husky voice calling in the night, "Mr. Finch? They gone?" Our nightmare had gone with daylight, everything would come out all right. (17.56)

Thought: In the controlled, familiar environment of the courtroom, Scout isn't scared, but Tom is as much in danger of his life there as he was that night in jail. What makes her feelings so different?

"I got somethin' to say an' then I ain't gonna say no more. That nigger yonder took advantage of me an' if you fine fancy gentlemen don't wanta do nothin' about it then you're all yellow stinkin' cowards, stinkin' cowards, the lot of you. Your fancy airs don't come to nothin' – your ma'amin' and Miss Mayellerin' don't come to nothin', Mr. Finch-" (18.167)

Thought: Why does Mayella choose "cowards" as her threat of choice for the men deciding her case? It's especially odd since more courage is required to go against the expected outcome and acquit Tom than to conform to community prejudice. Perhaps it's just what Mayella thinks is the worst thing you can call a man, but that raises the further question of why she would think that.

"You're very candid about this, why did you run so fast?"

"I says I was scared, suh."

"If you had a clear conscience, why were you scared?"

"Like I says before, it weren't safe for any nigger to be in a – fix like that."

"But you weren't in a fix – you testified that you were resisting Miss Ewell. Were you so scared that she'd hurt you, you ran, a big buck like you?"

"No suh, I's scared I'd be in court, just like I am now."

"Scared of arrest, scared you'd have to face up to what you did?"

"No suh, scared I'd hafta face up to what I didn't do." (19.141-148)

Thought: Tom's experience suggests that African-Americans in Maycomb have a whole additional set of fears to those of the white residents – and while Mr. Gilmer is trying to suggest that Tom didn't have any reason to be scared if he wasn't doing anything wrong, the very fact that Tom is in court on trial for his shows that his fears were very well-founded.

"In the second place, they're afraid. Then, they're-"

"Afraid, why?" asked Jem.

"Well, what if – say, Mr. Link Deas had to decide the amount of damages to award, say, Miss Maudie, when Miss Rachel ran over her with a car. Link wouldn't like the thought of losing either lady's business at his store, would he? So he tells Judge Taylor that he can't serve on the jury because he doesn't have anybody to keep store for him while he's gone. [...]

"Serving on a jury forces a man to make up his mind and declare himself about something. Men don't like to do that. Sometimes it's unpleasant." (23.47-52)

Thought: Atticus suggests that it's not just the actual fallout they would have to face from the community that keeps Maycomb's residents with background, as Miss Maudie would say, from serving on juries, but also fear of publicly taking a stand, even if it's on something they firmly believe in private. Perhaps this fear also influenced Tom's jury – even if they thought that no one would treat them any differently if they brought back a verdict of "not guilty," just declaring an opinion that goes against the common view is scary enough.

Mr. Ewell kept the same distance behind her until she reached Mr. Link Deas's house. All the way to the house, Helen said, she heard a soft voice behind her, crooning foul words. Thoroughly frightened, she telephoned Mr. Link at his store, which was not too far from his house. As Mr. Link came out of his store he saw Mr. Ewell leaning on the fence. Mr. Ewell said, "Don't you look at me, Link Deas, like I was dirt. I ain't jumped your-"

"First thing you can do, Ewell, is get your stinkin' carcass off my property. You're leanin' on it an' I can't afford fresh paint for it. Second thing you can do is stay away from my cook or I'll have you up for assault-"

"I ain't touched her, Link Deas, and ain't about to go with no nigger!"

"You don't have to touch her, all you have to do is make her afraid, an' if assault ain't enough to keep you locked up awhile, I'll get you in on the Ladies' Law, so get outa my sight! If you don't think I mean it, just bother that girl again!"

Mr. Ewell evidently thought he meant it, for Helen reported no further trouble. (27.8-12)

Thought: If Link Deas hadn't stepped in, the terrorist might have won – Helen might have been so creeped out by Ewell's behavior, and afraid that he would do something even worse if she stuck to business as usual, that she would have hid in her house or left Maycomb altogether. The effectiveness of his intervention suggests that for Ewell, it's all about power – by scaring Helen he's declaring his power over her, but Deas scaring him in turn makes him back off before someone more powerful than he is.

"It is a scary place though, ain't it?" I said. "Boo doesn't mean anybody any harm, but I'm right glad you're along." [...] "Ain't you scared of haints?"

We laughed. Haints, Hot Steams, incantations, secret signs, had vanished with our years as mist with sunrise. (28.3-7)

Thought: While Jem and Scout laugh at their childish fears, there are still real things to be scared of (as their upcoming encounter with Ewell makes clear) – fear itself isn't something to grow out of, just the causes of fear change as they get older.

"Read it out loud, please, Atticus. It's real scary."

"No," he said. "You've had enough scaring for a while. This is too-"

"Atticus, I wasn't scared."

He raised his eyebrows, and I protested: "Leastways not till I started telling Mr. Tate about it. Jem wasn't scared. Asked him and he said he wasn't. Besides, nothin's real scary except in books." (31.43-46)

Thought: Is Scout telling the truth about not being scared, or is this a white lie for Atticus's benefit, like Mr. Raymond's "drinking" for the sake of the citizens of Maycomb? Scout suggests that telling the story of scary events is more fear-inducing than actually living through them – which fits with her not getting upset about the lynch mob until after she was safe at home in bed and started thinking about what happened. But Atticus himself was scared in the present moment that night. Maybe this is another difference between adults and children, or perhaps it's just a quirk of the way Scout herself sees the world.

Women and Femininity Quotes

I was not so sure, but Jem told me I was being a girl, that girls always imagined things, that's why other people hated them so, and if I started behaving like one I could just go off and find some to play with. (4.119)

Thought: Scout believes from an early age that girl things are bad and boy things are good, and that she can avoid the badness of girls by not acting one. Being a girl for Scout is thus less a matter of what she's born with and more a matter of what she does.

"Scout, I'm tellin' you for the last time, shut your trap or go home – I declare to the Lord you're gettin' more like a girl every day!" With that, I had no option but to join them. (6.24)

Thought: Convinced of the unworthiness of girls, Scout will apparently do anything to avoid appearing like one.

"Don't pay any attention to her, just hold your head high and be a gentleman." (11.23)

Thought: This is the flip side of Jem's putting down of girls – being a gentleman seems to signify honor in a way being a lady doesn't, at least for Jem.

[Calpurnia] seemed glad to see me when I appeared in the kitchen, and by watching her I began to think there was some skill involved in being a girl. (12.8)

Thought: Until now, being a girl has been what happens when Scout fails to live up to Jem's standards of what a person should be. Watching Calpurnia, Scout realizes she might actually have to learn some things if she does want to be a girl, and that being a girl might even have some value.

I felt the starched walls of a pink cotton penitentiary closing in on me, and for the second time in my life I thought of running away. Immediately. (14.24)

Thought: This passage gives a striking image of how Scout sees girlhood – a prison that may look pretty from the outside, but which would hold her in, take away her freedom, and prevent her from doing what she really wants to do.

I walked home with Dill and returned in time to overhear Atticus saying to Aunty, "...in favor of Southern womanhood as much as anybody, but not for preserving polite fiction at the expense of human life," a pronouncement that made me suspect they had been fussing again. (15.39)

Thought: In calling Southern womanhood a "polite fiction," Atticus asserts that it's not real, it's just an idea that people at least pretend to believe in to make life run smoother. And what makes for a particularly Southern womanhood? How is being a woman in the south different from being a woman in the north?

"For one thing, Miss Maudie can't serve on a jury because she's a woman-"

"You mean women in Alabama can't-?" I was indignant.

"I do. I guess it's to protect our frail ladies from sordid cases like Tom's. Besides," Atticus grinned, "I doubt if we'd ever get a complete case tried – the ladies'd be interrupting to ask questions."

Jem and I laughed. Miss Maudie on a jury would be impressive. I thought of old Mrs. Dubose in her wheelchair – "Stop that rapping, John Taylor, I want to ask this man something." Perhaps our forefathers were wise. (23.43-46)

Thought: Perhaps this is part of the "polite fiction" Atticus was talking about before - – the belief that women are delicate and need to be protected, when really there's a fear that if they had more power they would use it in ways the men wouldn't like.

Ladies in bunches always filled me with vague apprehension and a firm desire to be elsewhere, but this feeling was what Aunt Alexandra called being "spoiled."

The ladies were cool in fragile pastel prints: most of them were heavily powdered but unrouged; the only lipstick in the room was Tangee Natural. Cutex Natural sparkled on their fingernails, but some of the younger ladies wore Rose. They smelled heavenly. I sat quietly, having conquered my hands by tightly gripping the arms of the chair, and waited for someone to speak to me. (24.13-14)

Thought: For being so fearful of ladies, Scout has amassed considerable knowledge about them, down to the brands of makeup they wear (perhaps that's the only kind available in Maycomb)? The level of detail in her description suggests that maybe Scout's just as fascinated as she is scared by these strange creatures.

There was no doubt about it, I must soon enter this world, where on its surface fragrant ladies rocked slowly, fanned gently, and drank cool water. But I was more at home in my father's world. People like Mr. Heck Tate did not trap you with innocent questions to make fun of you; even Jem was not highly critical unless you said something stupid. Ladies seemed to live in faint horror of men, seemed unwilling to approve wholeheartedly of them. But I liked them. There was something about them, no matter how much they cussed and drank and gambled and chewed; no matter how undelectable they were, there was something about them that I instinctively liked... they weren't –

"Hypocrites, Mrs. Perkins, born hypocrites," Mrs. Merriweather was saying. (24.54-55)

Thought: Mrs. Merriweather's spoken words, through the magic of literature, finish Scout's unspoken thought. At this point Scout feels like she understands men and their rules, and that she can trust them to behave in a certain way, whereas ladies are still a mystery. The idea of being "at home" in the male world is interesting, as if womanhood is an undiscovered country that Scout has to discover and map in order to make it her own.

Aunt Alexandra looked across the room at me and smiled. She looked at a tray of cookies on the table and nodded at them. I carefully picked up the tray and watched myself walk to Mrs. Merriweather. With my best company manners, I asked her if she would have some. After all, if Aunty could be a lady at a time like this, so could I. (24.93)

Thought: By this late point in the novel, being a lady has finally become something that Scout aspires to as a valued and worthwhile role. While on the one hand acting like everything is fine while Tom has just died may seem hypocritical, on the other it requires great strength to keep what should be private out of the public eye.

Family Quotes

"If Uncle Atticus lets you run around with stray dogs, that's his own business, like Grandma says, so it ain't your fault. I guess it ain't your fault if Uncle Atticus is a nigger-lover besides, but I'm here to tell you it certainly does mortify the rest of the family-"

"Francis, what the hell do you mean?"

"Just what I said. Grandma says it's bad enough he lets you all run wild, but now he's turned out a nigger-lover we'll never be able to walk the streets of Maycomb agin. He's ruinin' the family, that's what he's doin'." (9.96-98)

Thought: Here family seems like an excuse for telling people what to do – there's no real reason why Atticus's behavior should reflect on anyone but himself and perhaps the parents who raised him, but Aunt Alexandra seems to think it's her business. Although in Maycomb's family-based social system, her fear that the Finches' popularity will plummet may be well-founded.

After my bout with Cecil Jacobs when I committed myself to a policy of cowardice, word got around that Scout Finch wouldn't fight any more, her daddy wouldn't let her. This was not entirely correct: I wouldn't fight publicly for Atticus, but the family was private ground. I would fight anyone from a third cousin upwards tooth and nail. Francis Hancock, for example, knew that. (10.6)

Thought: While Atticus is the same in both public and private, Scout is not – she's willing to toe the line and play it cool with outsiders, but she still fights privately with her own family. Is it just Atticus's opinion that's the reason for the distinction, or is there some other difference?

Somewhere, I had received the impression that Fine Folks were people who did the best they could with the sense they had, but Aunt Alexandra was of the opinion, obliquely expressed, that the longer a family had been squatting on one patch of land the finer it was. (13.28)

Thought: Scout's definition of "Fine Folks" is based on what their actions are – something they have control over – while Aunt Alexandra's is based on their family history – something they can't help. Rags-to-riches stories don't impress her – she wants good solid staying-in-one-place-ness. While Scout's version allows people to get better through individual choice, in Aunt Alexandra's eyes quality is a function of time more than anything.

There was indeed a caste system in Maycomb, but to my mind it worked this way: the older citizens, the present generation of people who had lived side by side for years and years, were utterly predictable to one another: they took for granted attitudes, character shadings, even gestures, as having been repeated in each generation and refined by time. Thus the dicta No Crawford Minds His Own Business, Every Third Merriweather Is Morbid, The Truth Is Not in the Delafields, All the Bufords Walk Like That, were simply guides to daily living: never take a check from a Delafield without a discreet call to the bank; Miss Maudie Atkinson's shoulder stoops because she was a Buford; if Mrs. Grace Merriweather sips gin out of Lydia E. Pinkham bottles it's nothing unusual – her mother did the same. (13.32)

Thought: Family is destiny in Maycomb. While on the one hand this is limiting – there's no way for a person to be different from their parents – on the other, it allows people to indulge themselves without being judged because general opinion is that they can't help themselves.

Atticus's voice was even: "Alexandra, Calpurnia's not leaving this house until she wants to. You may think otherwise, but I couldn't have got along without her all these years. She's a faithful member of this family and you'll simply have to accept things the way they are." (14.28)

Thought: While Aunt Alexandra's idea of family is based on exclusivity – kicking out those who aren't worthy of being counted in – Atticus's is much more inclusive. Aunt Alexandra arranges family by blood, while Atticus considers affection and loyalty. Once again Aunt Alexandra thinks of family as what a person's born into, while Atticus thinks about whom that person connects with.

"Aunty," Jem spoke up, "Atticus says you can choose your friends but you sho' can't choose your family, an' they're still kin to you no matter whether you acknowledge 'em or not, and it makes you look right silly when you don't."

"That's your father all over again," said Aunt Alexandra, "and I still say that Jean Louise will not

invite Walter Cunningham to this house. If he were her double first cousin once removed he would still not be received in this house unless he comes to see Atticus on business. Now that is that." (23.84-85)

Thought: Here Atticus's and Aunt Alexandra's opinions appear to be switched – Atticus, as Jem quotes him, says that family is something you can't help, while Aunt Alexandra comes down on the side of choice. But in another sense their views haven't changed: Atticus is still concerned with keeping people in the family, while Aunt Alexandra wants to kick out the unworthy.

Atticus told me one time that most of this Old Family stuff's foolishness because everybody's family's just as old as everybody else's. I said did that include the colored folks and Englishmen and he said yes." "Background doesn't mean Old Family," said Jem. "I think it's how long your family's been readin' and writin'. Scout, I've studied this real hard and that's the only reason I can think of. Somewhere along when the Finches were in Egypt one of 'em must have learned a hieroglyphic or two and he taught his boy." Jem laughed. "Imagine Aunty being proud her great-grandaddy could read an' write – ladies pick funny things to be proud of." (23.41-42)

Thought: Once again Jem and Scout try to come up with a definition of Aunt Alexandra's mysterious term "background" that includes themselves but excludes all the people they know Aunt Alexandra thinks don't have it. Jem's focus on literacy here may have some truth to it – literacy means education, which means having a certain class and wealth status. Or perhaps the pride that Jem mentions in the last sentence is really the key – maybe "background" is just knowing that you're better than other people, and coming up with justifications for that after the fact. And what exactly is the relationship between "background" and "Old Family" and "family" more generally?

"I can't say I approve of everything he does, Maudie, but he's my brother, and I just want to know when this will ever end." Her voice rose: "It tears him to pieces. He doesn't show it much, but it tears him to pieces." (24.76)

Thought: For all Aunt Alexandra says about family in the abstract, she does really care about her actual family members, and isn't about to cast them out of the family circle even if they do things she doesn't agree with.

I learned more about the poor Mrunas' social life from listening to Mrs. Merriweather: they had so little sense of family that the whole tribe was one big family. A child had as many fathers as there were men in the community, as many mothers as there were women. J. Grimes Everett was doing his utmost to change this state of affairs, and desperately needed our prayers. (27.18)

Thought: What's so wrong with this picture of Mruna social life? Perhaps just that it's different, and doesn't involve putting people into neat little categories where it's easier to say this group is better than that other group.

"Heck," Atticus's back was turned. "If this thing's hushed up it'll be a simple denial to Jem of the way I've tried to raise him. Sometimes I think I'm a total failure as a parent, but I'm all they've got. Before Jem looks at anyone else he looks at me, and I've tried to live so I can look squarely back at him... if I connived at something like this, frankly I couldn't meet his eye, and the day I can't do that I'll know I've lost him. I don't want to lose him and Scout, because they're all I've got." (30.37)

Thought: Atticus seems much less concerned with judging his children (as opposed to, say, Bob Ewell) than with how they might judge him. How dependent is Atticus's good behavior on his children? Would he behave differently if they didn't exist? If not, why does he so often refer to them when he's trying to explain to others why he acts like he does?

Compassion and Forgiveness Quotes

"First of all," he said, "if you can learn a simple trick, Scout, you'll get along a lot better with all kinds of folks. You never really understand a person until you consider things from his point of view [...] until you climb into his skin and walk around in it." (3.85-87)

Thought: Atticus's advice "to climb into someone's skin and walk around in it" sounds rather more gruesome than just walking a mile in someone's shoes, but the idea is the same: compassion is based on sympathy, on being able to put yourself in the other person's place and understand why they act the way they do even if you don't agree with it. Or is more required – is it possible to understand someone and still not feel compassion for them?

"This time we aren't fighting the Yankees, we're fighting our friends. But remember this, no matter how bitter things get, they're still our friends and this is still our home." (9.27)

Thought: If you're engaged in bitter warfare with someone, can you still be their friend at the same time? According to Atticus, you can – either because you continue to treat them with a friend's respect, or because they're part of a larger community that stays whole even if its parts are pulling in different directions.

"Scout," said Atticus, "when summer comes you'll have to keep your head about far worse things... it's not fair for you and Jem, I know that, but sometimes we have to make the best of things, and the way we conduct ourselves when the chips are down – well, all I can say is, when you and Jem are grown, maybe you'll look back on this with some compassion and some feeling that I didn't let you down." (11.53)

Thought: Atticus knows that his behavior seems incomprehensible or just plain stupid from some perspectives, so he hopes Scout and Jem will be able to understand why he did what he did when they're older, even if they're too young to get it now. This quote suggests that Atticus sees no shame in being the object of compassion, in fact that it's something to hope for.

Suddenly Mayella became articulate. "I got somethin' to say," she said.

Atticus raised his head. "Do you want to tell us what happened?" But she did not hear the compassion in his invitation. (18.165-166)

Thought: Mayella's inability even to recognize Atticus's politeness or compassion for her shows just how different her world is from his – neither is something she's had any experience with, and so they're strange to her.

"Yes, suh. I felt right sorry for her, she seemed to try more'n the rest of 'em-"

"You felt sorry for her, you felt sorry for her?" Mr. Gilmer seemed ready to rise to the ceiling. The witness realized his mistake and shifted uncomfortably in the chair. But the damage was done. Below us, nobody liked Tom Robinson's answer. Mr. Gilmer paused a long time to let it sink in. (19.125-126)

Thought: Why is Tom's compassion for Mayella such a problem? Perhaps it's because feeling sorry for someone implies that you think they're worse off than you are – and in racially-divided Maycomb, for any African-American person to think he's superior to any white person is seriously messing with the order of things.

"Jem, see if you can stand in Bob Ewell's shoes a minute. I destroyed his last shred of credibility at that trial, if he had any to begin with. The man had to have some kind of comeback, his kind always does. So if spitting in my face and threatening me saved Mayella Ewell one extra beating, that's something I'll gladly take. He had to take it out on somebody and I'd rather it be me than that houseful of children out there. You understand?" (23.15)

Thought: Perhaps Atticus really is so selflessly good that he can feel compassion even for Bob Ewell. Or perhaps compassion really is based on a sense of superiority – Atticus can afford to be so generous because he knows he's so much better off than the Ewells will ever be, just because he was born a Finch instead of a Ewell. Or could both options be true at the same time?

"Oh child, those poor Mrunas," she said, and was off. Few other questions would be necessary.

Mrs. Merriweather's large brown eyes always filled with tears when she considered the oppressed. "Living in that jungle with nobody but J. Grimes Everett," she said. "Not a white person'll go near 'em but that saintly J. Grimes Everett."

Mrs. Merriweather played her voice like an organ; every word she said received its full measure: "The poverty... the darkness... the immorality – nobody but J. Grimes Everett knows." (24.26-28)

Thought: "The oppressed" get Mrs. Merriweather's compassion, but her maid Sophy doesn't. And even here it seems that Mrs. Merriweather cares much more about J. Grimes Everett than she does about the Mrunas themselves. While Mrs. Merriweather may talk about compassion, and believe that she herself is a compassionate person, her home life and actions suggest otherwise. Mrs. Merriweather suggests that while compassion is relatively easy in the abstract, actually living it is much more difficult.

"There's one thing I truly believe, Gertrude," she continued, "but some people just don't see it my way. If we just let them know we forgive 'em, that we've forgotten it, then this whole thing'll blow over." (24.40)

Thought: While Atticus talks about seeing things through other people's eyes, Mrs. Merriweather wants everyone not only to try her skin on but agree that she is right. Her unthinking insistence that the African-Americans need to be forgiven (for what?), rather than being the ones doing the forgiving of Mrs. Merriweather and her ilk, shows that Mrs. Merriweather's compassion is so one-sided as to be hardly compassionate at all.

[Jem] was certainly never cruel to animals, but I had never known his charity to embrace the insect world.

"Why couldn't I mash him?" I asked.

"Because they don't bother you," Jem answered in the darkness. He had turned out his reading light.

"Reckon you're at the stage now where you don't kill flies and mosquitoes now, I reckon," I said. "Lemme know when you change your mind. Tell you one thing, though, I ain't gonna sit around and not scratch a redbug."

"Aw dry up," he answered drowsily.

Jem was the one who was getting more like a girl every day, not I. (24.7-12)

Thought: Scout's words here suggest that compassion is a feminine quality, which seems odd since most of her lessons in compassion have come from Atticus. Perhaps the larger cultural message that feelings are by default female trumps her own personal experience in the way she thinks about the issue. In any case, she's using the idea that "compassion" equals "girl" in order to assert that "girl" definitely does not equal "Scout."

I looked behind me. To the left of the brown door was a long shuttered window. I walked to it, stood in front of it, and turned around. In daylight, I thought, you could see to the postoffice corner. [...]

Atticus was right. One time he said you never really know a man until you stand in his shoes and walk around in them. Just standing on the Radley porch was enough. (31.25-31)

Thought: Here the metaphor of "seeing" becomes literal – Scout actually stands on the Radley porch and imagines what Boo has seen over the last few years. And what Boo has seen – the life and times of Jem and Scout – has made him feel compassion for them, and come to their rescue when they needed it. Are the two processes – seeing someone and imagining what someone else sees – different in how they produce compassion? What is it about seeing in particular that sparks compassionate feelings? What are the middle steps between sight and compassion?

Plot Analysis

Classic Plot Analysis

Initial Situation
The Finches are part of the Maycomb community.
This is where the story begins, and also the base state that gets disrupted and questioned as the story progresses. The place of the Finches in Maycomb, and how their views relate to the views of their fellow townspeople, is what gets complicated and eventually resolved through the plot.

Conflict
Atticus Finch agrees to defend the black man Tom Robinson on charges of raping a white woman, even though public opinion is against him.
This battle – between Atticus's desire to give Tom the best defense possible and other people's desire to preserve the status quo – fuels a lot of the smaller conflicts between Scout and her peers.

Complication
In court Atticus makes a strong case that the Ewells are lying and Tom is innocent.
The trial makes it obvious that Atticus is right and his opposition is wrong – so it's up to the jury to side either with justice or with the racist status quo.

Climax
The jury finds Tom Robinson guilty.
The status quo wins. Despite Atticus's best efforts, and Jem's belief that the people of Maycomb couldn't do something so fundamentally wrong as send an innocent man to the electric chair, the jury convicts Tom. Everything in the novel leads to this point, and nothing is

the same for the Finches afterwards.

Suspense
Mr. Ewell threatens Atticus and harasses Helen Robinson.
Suspense is often linked with fear, and in this part of the novel both Jem and Scout are very afraid that Mr. Ewell is going to do something to Atticus.

Denouement
Mr. Ewell attacks Jem and Scout.
Mr. Ewell finally strikes, ending the suspense, but unexpectedly Atticus is not his victim – he targets Jem and Scout instead, but gets killed in the process.

Conclusion
Scout finally meets Boo Radley.
In a way this is another climax, since the book has been talking about Boo from the first page, and he doesn't actually appear until almost the end. But it's also the resolution, as Scout finally leaves behind the fears and fantasies of her childhood in which Boo plays a part, in order to see him as a real person.

Booker's Seven Basic Plots Analysis: Tragedy

Anticipation Stage
Tom waits in jail for his trial to begin, knowing that even though he's got the best defense attorney in Maycomb, he's still 99.99% sure to be convicted.
Tom's in a holding pattern – there's nothing he can do about his situation until the trial starts.

Dream Stage
Atticus, with Scout's help, protects Tom from a lynch mob.
Scout's intervention manages to change a man's mind, raising the hope that Atticus might be able to do the same with the jury.

Frustration Stage
Atticus makes his case in court so strongly that it's obvious Tom is innocent, but white public opinion is against him.
Atticus puts forth a strong case, but Ewell's appeal to prejudice has a stronger effect.

Nightmare Stage
Despite Atticus's best efforts to prove Tom's innocence, the jury still finds him guilty and sentences him to death.
All hopes are dashed, and the disappointment is sharp. Tom loses hope and falls into despair.

Destruction or Death Wish Stage
Without hope that an appeal will change the verdict, Tom attempts a foolhardy prison break and is killed.
Tom still has a chance on appeal, but is tired of waiting around for others to decide his fate, so,

consciously or unconsciously, he decides for himself to end it.

Three Act Plot Analysis

Act I
Atticus makes it clear to Maycomb that he's going to defend Tom Robinson to the best of his ability.

Act II
The Robinson case goes to trial and the jury finds Tom guilty.

Act III
Ewell attacks the Finch children and dies; Scout meets Boo Radley.

Study Questions

1. The events of *To Kill a Mockingbird* are set in the 1930s, but racism is still with us – for example, just a few years ago, African-American students at a Southern high school were harassed for sitting under a tree unofficially reserved for white students and then prosecuted for fighting back against their tormentors (they became known as the Jena Six). What can the novel tell us about facing racism today?
2. How do gender and race intersect in the novel? How much of Mayella's treatment is due not just to her being a white person accusing an African-American, but a white woman accusing an African-American man?
3. After *To Kill a Mockingbird*, Harper Lee never wrote another novel. If she had written a sequel continuing Scout's story, what might it be like?
4. How would the novel be different if it were narrated from Jem's perspective? Atticus's? Calpurnia's? Or in the third person?
5. Many lawyers credit Atticus as their inspiration for entering the law profession, but others criticize that he's portrayed in the novel as the lone protector of powerless African-Americans who can't do anything for themselves. To what extent can Atticus be taken as a role model?
6. Why do so many of the characters have nicknames?

Characters

All Characters

Jean Louise Finch (Scout) Character Analysis

Scout's Honor

Scout may or may not be a lover, but she's definitely a fighter. Especially at the beginning of the novel, fighting is her solution to everything: she goes after Walter Cunningham after she gets in trouble on his behalf on the first day of school, she beats up Dill when she thinks he's not paying enough attention to her, and she kicks a member of the lynch mob (in the balls, no less) when he grabs Jem. When news of Atticus's defense of Tom Robinson percolates down to the schoolyard, it's no wonder that she responds with her fists to the kids' parroting of their parents' insults.

Why is violence almost always Scout's first response? Well, for one thing, she does seem to win her fights most of the time, so it's a technique that's working for her. For another, if might makes right, then it skips over the trickier business of thinking about the moral right: righteousness goes to whomever is the better fighter. Scout's fighting shows her quick temper and lack of self-control, but it also suggests her simplicity when it comes to moral matters, and her desire for a quick fix to complicated questions.

While Scout doesn't see a problem with her Mortal Kombat approach to dealing with people, Atticus thinks otherwise, and tells Scout not to fight any more. Scout has difficulty obeying him, but manages it at least some of the time, starting with her classmate Cecil Jacobs.

I drew a bead on him, remembered what Atticus had said, then dropped my fists and walked away, "Scout's a cow- ward!" ringing in my ears. It was the first time I ever walked away from a fight.

Somehow, if I fought Cecil I would let Atticus down. Atticus so rarely asked Jem and me to do something for him, I could take being called a coward for him. I felt extremely noble for having remembered, and remained noble for three weeks. (9.30-31)

And so Scout learns the pleasure of moral superiority, though she does eventually understand that there are more reasons against fighting than obedience to Atticus and getting to feel noble. Even then, however, she does maintain a few private exceptions.

After my bout with Cecil Jacobs when I committed myself to a policy of cowardice, word got around that Scout Finch wouldn't fight any more, her daddy wouldn't let her. This was not entirely correct: I wouldn't fight publicly for Atticus, but the family was private ground. I would fight anyone from a third cousin upwards tooth and nail. (10.6)

Why will Scout not fight Cecil, whom she has to see every day, but will fight Francis, whom she sees only a few times a year? Perhaps it has to do with her desire to do right by Atticus – fighting her schoolmates would be publicly going against his command, while hauling off at Francis is all in the family, so to speak.

Scout as Tomboy

As all this fighting suggests, Scout doesn't have much interest in stereotypical girl things, like dolls and dresses. Her tomboyish nature drives her prim Aunt Alexandra crazy, and Aunty comes to stay with her brother and his family in part to try to make a proper little girl out of Scout, which means first of all giving up her overalls.

Aunt Alexandra was fanatical on the subject of my attire. I could not possibly hope to be a lady if I wore breeches; when I said I could do nothing in a dress, she said I wasn't supposed to be doing things that required pants. Aunt Alexandra's vision of my deportment involved playing with small stoves, tea sets, and wearing the Add-A-Pearl necklace she gave me when I was born; furthermore, I should be a ray of sunshine in my father's lonely life . (9.74)

Scout takes Aunt Alexandra's crusade against her pants as also against her freedom, and she doesn't seem too far off. For Scout, being a lady-in-training means giving up all the things she likes to do and replacing them with what others expect her to do, and Scout is having none of it: "I felt the starched walls of a pink cotton penitentiary closing in on me, and for the second time in my life I thought of running away" (17.24).

While Scout doesn't ever renounce her tomboyish ways, she does come to recognize that being a lady has some value. When Aunt Alexandra puts her game face on to return to her tea party after hearing of Tom's death, Scout takes pride in following her lead: "After all, if Aunty could be a lady at a time like this, so could I" (24.93). While she still isn't comfortable with the rules ladies have to follow and the skills they have to cultivate, Scout does pick up on the examples of the strong women in her life (not only the formidable Aunt Alexandra, but also her sharp-tongued, no-nonsense neighbor Miss Maudie) to make some kind of peace with her gender.

Boo Radley and Scout's Coming of Age

From the beginning, Scout is more terrified of Boo than Jem or Dill are. While the two older boys push at the edges of their fears by attempting to make indirect contact with Boo, Scout hangs back, not wanting to bring the monster's wrath down upon them. When she does get drawn into their schemes, she pays for it with sleepless nights.

Every night-sound I heard from my cot on the back porch was magnified three-fold; every scratch of feet on gravel was Boo Radley seeking revenge, every passing Negro laughing in the night was Boo Radley loose and after us; insects splashing against the screen were Boo Radley's insane fingers picking the wire to pieces; the chinaberry trees were malignant, hovering, alive. (6.84)

In Scout's fevered mind, Boo expands into a dangerous world, where every sound signals a threat. And later, when Scout realizes that it was Boo who brought her a blanket, she's nearly sick, as if realizing that she had just walked along the edge of a cliff in the dark and only survived by chance. While part of Scout's fear of Boo she shares with any kid who ever thought there was a monster under the bed, it also seems linked to a fear of unknown dangers lurking in the seemingly familiar.

As time passes and Scout faces down more real threats, her fear of Boo lessens. He lurks in her imagination not as a monster but as a neighbor, who feels familiar even though she's never actually laid eyes on him.

But I still looked for him each time I went by. Maybe someday we would see him. I imagined how it would be: when it happened, he'd just be sitting in the swing when I came along. "Hidy do, Mr. Arthur," I would say, as if I had said it every afternoon of my life. "Evening, Jean Louise," he would say, as if he had said it every afternoon of my life, "right pretty spell we're having, isn't it?" "Yes sir, right pretty," I would say, and go on.It was only a fantasy. (26.5-6)

This shift in Scout's interest in Boo reflects her growing experience with different kinds of people; having seen the likes of Bob Ewell, poor Boo doesn't offer much in the way of chills anymore. Having faced the evil of real people, perhaps Scout doesn't see the unknown as scary in itself. Or perhaps her changing view of Boo has something to do with post-trial shifts in her ideas about community, and what makes for good neighbors.

When Scout finally does meet Boo, it causes yet more upheaval in how she thinks about not only him and her community, but also herself.

Neighbors bring food with death and flowers with sickness and little things in between. Boo was our neighbor. He gave us two soap dolls, a broken watch and chain, a pair of good-luck pennies, and our lives. But neighbors give in return. We never put back into the tree what we took out of it: we had given him nothing, and it made me sad. (31.23)

Seeing Boo makes Scout see herself differently, and she's not entirely pleased with what she sees. This moment of self-examination suggests that Atticus stopped too soon with his advice that putting yourself in another person's shoes allows you to understand them better – it also has the potential to let you understand yourself.

While Scout may be exaggerating a bit when she thinks, "as I made my way home, I thought Jem and I would get grown but there wasn't much else left for us to learn, except possibly algebra" (31.31) – what about calculus? – she has learned a great deal, not just this evening, but over the four years of the book. The question is, what will she do with this knowledge? What kind of person will it enable her to become?

Jean Louise Finch (Scout) Timeline and Summary

- Scout lives on a main street in Maycomb.
- Her mother died when she was two.

- The summer Scout is five, she meets Dill.
- That fall, she starts school, and gets in trouble for knowing how to read.
- She tries to explain to the teacher why Walter Cunningham doesn't have a lunch, but gets in trouble for that too.
- At recess she beats Walter up, but Jem steps in and invites Walter home for lunch.
- When Walter pours molasses all over his food, Scout asks him what he's doing, and gets scolded by Calpurnia.
- All in all, Scout's first day of school makes her want never to return, but Atticus convinces her that she has to go back.
- One day on her way home from school Scout finds some chewing gum hidden in a tree in front of the Radley Place.
- On the last day of school, Scout and Jem find a box containing two Indian-head pennies in the same tree.
- Dill arrives for the summer, and Scout tells him Jem is just making up his stories about Hot Steams.
- In revenge Jem gives Scout an extra push when she's riding inside an old tire, and she lands right in the Radleys' front yard.
- A dazed Scout runs out of there as fast as she can, leaving Jem to retrieve the tire.
- Despite being uneasy about the whole thing, Scout joins with Jem and Scout in acting out scenes from Boo Radley's life.
- Scout really wants to quit the game for two reasons: one, Atticus caught them and told them to stop, and two, when her tire dumped her in front of the Radley Place she heard someone laughing inside.
- Scout passes many of her evenings hanging out with neighbor Miss Maudie on her porch.
- Miss Maudie tells Scout about Boo Radley and foot-washing Baptists.
- Scout finds out that Jem and Dill are still trying to get Boo Radley to come out, but joins in when Jem calls her a girl for objecting.
- Scout accompanies the boys on their midnight raid of the Radley Place, and waits at home in terror when Jem has to return for his pants.
- Scout and Jem keep finding treasures in the tree, until Nathan Radley fills the hole with cement.
- Scout and Jem have a rare snow day off from school and build a snow man.
- Atticus wakes Scout up in the middle of the night: Miss Maudie's house is on fire.
- Scout watches the doomed efforts to save the house from a safe spot in front of the Radley Place.
- When she returns home after the fire is out, she gets a surprise: she's wearing a blanket she didn't have when she left, and the only person who could have draped it around her is Boo Radley.
- At school, Scout fights Cecil Jacobs for calling Atticus names.
- Atticus hears about it and tells her not to get into fights on his behalf.
- At Christmas, Scout and Jem look forward to seeing Uncle Jack but dread spending time at Aunt Alexandra's.
- Scout fights her cousin Francis because he insulted Atticus and gets in trouble with Uncle Jack.
- Later she convinces Uncle Jack to listen to her side of the story.
- When he hears what Scout has to say, Uncle Jack wants to go take on Francis himself, but Scout makes him promise not to tell anyone, not even Atticus.

- Scout eavesdrops on Uncle Jack and Atticus talking about the Robinson case, but Jack doesn't make a peep about Scout's fighting ways.
- Scout and Jem feel bad that their father can't do anything interesting or impressive.
- Scout talks to Miss Maudie about it, but she doesn't change her mind.
- Scout and Jem see a mad dog coming down the street, and watch as Atticus shoots it.
- Scout wants to brag to everyone about how her father is a good shot, but Jem tells her not to.
- Jem buys Scout a baton, but he breaks it destroying Mrs. Dubose's camellias after the old woman insults Atticus.
- Scout talks to Atticus about why he's defending Tom Robinson.
- Scout accompanies Jem as he performs his penance: reading aloud to Mrs. Dubose every day after school.
- Jem's getting older, and Scout's having more difficulty understanding him.
- Scout is miserable when Dill doesn't turn up in Maycomb for the summer.
- With Atticus away on a Sunday, Calpurnia takes Scout and Jem to her own, African-American, church.
- Seeing Calpurnia at her own church prompts Scout and Jem to ask her questions about herself.
- Scout and Jem arrive home to find Aunt Alexandra on the front porch.
- Scout doesn't like Aunt Alexandra and the way she tries to make her niece into a lady.
- Scout, after hearing cryptic town gossip, asks Atticus what rape is, and he explains.
- Scout wants to visit Calpurnia at home, but Aunt Alexandra puts her foot down and says No.
- After stepping on something strange, Scout finds Dill hiding under her bed.
- Scout talks to Dill and tries to understand why he ran away from his family.
- Scout and Jem watch as Atticus talks with a group of men who arrive on their doorstep one night, concerned about the Tom Robinson case.
- The next night, Jem goes out, and Scout joins him.
- Picking up Dill along the way, they go to the town square looking for Atticus.
- The trio sees him sitting in front of the jail reading, and are about to leave when some men drive up.
- While Atticus is talking to the men, Scout runs up to join them.
- Scout is surprised and embarrassed to find that they are different men from last night, men she doesn't know.
- One of the men grabs Jem, and Scout kicks him.
- While Jem and Atticus face off over whether the kids will stay or go, Scout starts talking to the one face she does recognize in the crowd, Mr. Cunningham.
- Mr. Cunningham doesn't respond to Scout's attempts to chat at first, but when she mentions his son and her classmate Walter, he talks to her a bit and then leaves with the rest of the men.
- Scout's not scared until she goes home and goes to bed, and then she starts crying.
- The next morning, Scout, Jem, and Dill watch the crowds on the way to the courthouse for Tom's trial.
- They go to the courthouse themselves, but the only seats they can get are in the balcony where the African-Americans sit.
- Scout watches the trial until Dill starts crying and Jem makes her take him out of the room.
- With Dill, she talks to Mr. Dolph Raymond, who is also outside the courthouse.

- Scout and Dill return inside to hear Atticus's closing remarks.
- After he finishes, Atticus finds out the kids are there, and sends them home for dinner.
- After dinner Scout, Jem, and Dill return, to find the jury still out.
- Scout dozes for a bit, but wakes up to hear the verdict: guilty.
- Reverend Sykes tells Scout to stand up, as the African-Americans are doing, as her father leaves the courtroom.
- The next day, Scout, Jem, and Dill try to avoid their adult neighbors, but join Miss Maudie for cake.
- After Bob Ewell spits in Atticus's face and threatens him, Scout and Jem are scared he will make good on his threats.
- Scout wants to hang out with Walter Cunningham, but Aunt Alexandra tells her she can't, which makes her mad.
- When Aunt Alexandra throws a tea party, Scout joins the ladies, who both attract and repel her.
- Miss Stephanie makes fun of Scout, but Miss Maudie gives her silent support.
- Atticus comes home and calls Aunt Alexandra to the kitchen, and Scout follows to hear that Tom Robinson has been shot and killed while trying to escape from prison.
- After Atticus leaves with Calpurnia to tell Helen Robinson, Scout joins Aunt Alexandra in keeping up appearances at the tea party.
- Scout starts third grade, which means passing the Radley Place every day.
- Scout's no longer scared of Boo, but still kind of would like to see him.
- At school, Scout is confused why her teacher Miss Gates criticizes Hitler but supports Tom's conviction.
- Scout is cast as a ham in the school's Halloween pageant.
- Jem walks Scout through the darkness to the school.
- On the way, Cecil Jacobs jumps out at Scout and Jem and scares them.
- Backstage at the pageant, Scout falls asleep, misses her cue, and enters late.
- To shield her embarrassment, Scout keeps her costume on so no one can see her, and waits with Jem until everyone else leaves.
- On their way home, Scout and Jem are attacked by someone, but Scout can't see anything because of her costume.
- A stranger picks up the unconscious Jem and carries him home while Scout follows.
- Scout is worried that Jem is dead, but Dr. Reynolds reassures her that he's not dead yet, and in fact is getting better.
- Mr. Tate arrives, tells them Ewell is dead at the scene of the crime, and asks Scout to tell them what happened.
- Scout tells what she knows, but she can't say how Ewell got stabbed.
- Scout finds out who the stranger is: it's Boo.
- Scout sits with Boo while Tate and Atticus argue over what to do, and then walks him home.
- Scout looks at her neighborhood from the new perspective of the Radleys' front porch.
- Scout returns home to fall asleep while Atticus reads to her.

Jeremy Atticus Finch (Jem) Character Analysis

Obsession with Boo

While Dill is often the imagination behind the Finch kids' early attempts to draw out Boo Radley, Jem is the one who takes action on his schemes. He's the one who overcomes his fear to run up and touch the Radleys' front door, fiddles with the fishing pole to try to leave a note on Boo's windowsill, and spearheads the midnight raid on the Radley Place. Why does Jem want to see Boo so badly? Perhaps it's just because he's there – a mystery right before their eyes. Or perhaps it's all a game – after all, it's Jem who comes up with the idea of acting out Boo's life, and takes on the starring role himself.

But it seems that Jem takes the Boo boondoggle more seriously than that. When Mr. Nathan cements up the hole in the tree in front of the Radley Place where the kids have been finding treasures, Jem is seriously upset.

Next morning on the way to school he ran ahead of me and stopped at the tree. Jem was facing me when he looked up, and I saw him go stark white.

"Scout!"

I ran to him.

Someone had filled our knot-hole with cement.

"Don't you cry, now, Scout... don't cry now, don't you worry-" he muttered at me all the way to school. (7.62-66)

Later Scout sees that Jem himself has been crying. It's not certain that Jem suspects Boo has been the one leaving them gifts, but that would give one reason why Jem is so distressed at having the connection with their Mystery Friend so abruptly cut off.

Relationship with Scout

As older brother to Scout, Jem looks out for her and tries to get her to do what he, in his superior knowledge from being four years older, knows she should do. Asserting Scout's inferiority, as younger and a girl, appears to be one way that Jem boosts his own ego. The Boo Radley play-acting game starts out as one of these ego-boosts.

"I know what we are going to play," he announced. "Something new, something different. [...] Boo Radley."

Jem's head at times was transparent: he had thought that up to make me understand he wasn't afraid of Radleys in any shape or form, to contrast his own fearless heroism with my cowardice. (4.82-85)

Scout knows what he's up to, but lets him get away with it. Jem's thoughts aren't always so clear to Scout, and they get more confusing to her as both kids get older. This means that Scout narrates what Jem says and does when he's around her, but she can't always identify what's going on inside his brain.

Jem stayed moody and silent for a week. As Atticus had once advised me to do, I tried to climb into Jem's skin and walk around in it: if I had gone alone to the Radley Place at two in the morning, my funeral would have been held the next afternoon. So I left Jem alone and tried not to bother him. (7.1)

Jem phases into and out of wanting to hang out with Scout; during the "on" periods, he takes on the role of her teacher whether she wants him to or not.

"That's because you can't hold something in your mind but a little while," said Jem. "It's different with grown folks, we-"

His maddening superiority was unbearable these days. He didn't want to do anything but read and go off by himself. Still, everything he read he passed along to me, but with this difference: formerly, because he thought I'd like it; now, for my edification and instruction. (14.41-42)

Is this just Jem asserting his superiority all over again? Or does he want to make sure his sister has as much useful knowledge at her fingertips as possible? Perhaps, just as before he cemented his identity as a brave boy through criticizing Scout as a weak girl, treating Scout as a child is a way for him to establish himself as a grown-up.

Relationship with Atticus

Early in the novel, Jem seems happy to dance around the edges of Atticus's rules.

He still maintained, however, that Atticus hadn't said we couldn't, therefore we could; and if Atticus ever said we couldn't, Jem had thought of a way around it: he would simply change the names of the characters and then we couldn't be accused of playing anything. (5.1)

Like a slick lawyer who follows the letter of the law but violates the spirit, Jem knows that Atticus wouldn't approve of their playacting Boo's life, but hopes he can wriggle out of it through plausible deniability.

When the stakes are raised after the midnight raid on the Radley Place, however, Jem thinks differently about Atticus finding out about this new torment to the Radleys. Scout thinks a beating from their father is better than risking getting shot by Mr. Radley, but Jem explains why he has to risk it.

I was desperate: "Look, it ain't worth it, Jem. A lickin' hurts but it doesn't last. You'll get your head shot off, Jem. Please..."

He blew out his breath patiently. "I – it's like this, Scout," he muttered. "Atticus ain't ever whipped me since I can remember. I wanta keep it that way. [...] We shouldn'a done that tonight, Scout." (6.97-98)

While Scout thinks it's better to face your punishment and get it over with, Jem would rather walk through fire than have the shame of giving Atticus a reason to be disappointed in him. (Of course, we find out later that Atticus knew all along, even though he didn't let on – perhaps he wants to give Jem a chance to redeem himself.)

But sometimes Jem's proud desire to defend Atticus overcomes his wish for his father's approval. Jem's most dramatic failure of gentlemanly behavior is his assault on Mrs. Dubose's camellias after hearing one too many insults from her on Atticus's moral character.

I sometimes wondered exactly what made Jem do it, what made him break the bonds of "You just be a gentleman, son," and the phase of self-conscious rectitude he had recently entered. Jem had probably stood as much guff about Atticus lawing for niggers as had I, and I took it for granted that he kept his temper – he had a naturally tranquil disposition and a slow fuse. At the time, however, I thought the only explanation for what he did was that for a few minutes he simply went mad. (11.29)

Perhaps Jem saw this as a way to get revenge on an ugly world through taking his rage out on things, rather than people. Faced with a person, Jem can hold himself back, but faced with an empty porch and a garden full of camellias, he's like someone looking at a sandcastle after the obnoxious kids who built it have left – total annihilation feels too satisfying to resist.

Jem, however, still has to face up to what he did, and Mrs. Dubose extracts every morsel of the pound of flesh she demands in retribution, and then some. Jem resists Atticus's commands first to apologize to Mrs. Dubose and then to agree to her demand that he read to her, but he obeys, and never again shows his anger at Mrs. Dubose's words. Atticus's response – putting Jem right back in the situation that got him into trouble in the first place, listening to Mrs. Dubose – shows his trust that Jem will do better in future, which Jem does his best to live up to.

While Jem stops attacking on Atticus's behalf, he does dig in at taking defensive action. At the Maycomb jail on the night the lynch mob shows up, Jem is the one who leads to kids downtown to check on Atticus; while Scout is the first to get them directly involved, it's Jem who point-blank refuses Atticus's command to leave.

We were accustomed to prompt, if not always cheerful acquiescence to Atticus's instructions, but from the way he stood Jem was not thinking of budging.

"Go home, I said."

Jem shook his head. As Atticus's fists went to his hips, so did Jem's, and as they faced each other I could see little resemblance between them: Jem's soft brown hair and eyes, his oval face and snug-fitting ears were our mother's, contrasting oddly with Atticus's graying black hair and square-cut features, but they were somehow alike. Mutual defiance made them alike. (15.96-98)

While at first Jem usually accepts what Atticus wants him to do as what's right, here the two sides – right and Atticus – diverge for him. Through his admiration of Atticus, Jem has learned to act with honor, but not necessarily with obedience, and here he puts honor first – through doing the same thing Atticus is doing, risking himself without much concern for how much that scares the people who love him.

Reaction to the Trial

Tom Robinson's trial is a watershed moment for Jem's character. Throughout the trial, Jem watches with great interest, and is convinced that based on the evidence, there is no way the jury can convict Tom. So when the verdict comes back as guilty, Jem feels as though he's been physically attacked.

Judge Taylor was polling the jury: "Guilty... guilty... guilty... guilty..." I peeked at Jem: his hands were white from gripping the balcony rail, and his shoulders jerked as if each "guilty" was a separate stab between them. (21.50)

While Jem's certainty about the trial's outcome is receiving these blows, the verdict also seems to be a broader attack on things Jem thought were true: that the legal system is just, that innocent men are acquitted, that Maycomb is a community of good, fair-minded people. After the trial, Jem struggles to figure out why people are so eager to divide into groups and hate each other. Scout says that people are just people, but Jem isn't so sure.

"That's what I thought, too," he said at last, "when I was your age. If there's just one kind of folks, why can't they get along with each other? If they're all alike, why do they go out of their way to despise each other? Scout, I think I'm beginning to understand something. I think I'm beginning to understand why Boo Radley's stayed shut up in the house all this time... it's because he wants to stay inside." (23.117)

The Tom Robinson trial makes Jem lose his faith in humanity. Will he ever get it back? Is there a way to acknowledge all the evil people do and be able still leave the house? (Atticus might have something to say about that.) Jem is unconscious for the conclusion of the novel, so he doesn't have the same moment of revelation that Scout does, but perhaps his waking up will also be a kind of rebirth.

Jeremy Atticus Finch (Jem) Timeline and Summary

- The summer Jem is nine, he meets Dill.
- Jem tells Dill scary stories about Boo Radley
- Dill dares Jem to go up to the Radley Place; Jem is scared, but he can't turn down a dare.
- Jem walks Scout to school on her first day.
- At recess, Jem tries to explain to Scout about the school's new system of education.
- Jem steps in when Scout is fighting with Walter Cunningham and invites the boy home for lunch.
- On the last day of school, Scout and Jem find a box containing two Indian-head pennies in the same tree.
- Dill arrives for the summer, and Jem tells him stories about Hot Steams, even though

Scout says he's just making them up.

- In revenge Jem gives Scout an extra push when she's riding inside an old tire, and she lands right in the Radleys' front yard.
- A dazed Scout runs out of there as fast as she can, leaving Jem to retrieve the tire.
- Jem ropes an enthusiastic Dill and a reluctant Scout into a new game: acting out scenes from Boo Radley's life.
- Jem keeps concocting plans for getting Boo to come out: first he tries to give him a note, then he tries to sneak up to the house at night, but he still doesn't see Boo.
- After the botched midnight raid on the Radley Place with Scout and Dill, Jem returns alone to retrieve his pants, which were caught on a fence.
- He finds his pants neatly folded on the fence, with the tear mended.
- Scout and Jem keep finding treasures in the tree, until Nathan Radley fills the hole with cement, which upsets Jem.
- Scout and Jem have a rare snow day off from school and build a snow man.
- The night Miss Maudie's house burns, Jem stands with Scout in front of the Radley Place, but he doesn't see Boo bring out the blanket for Scout either.
- At Christmas, Scout and Jem look forward to seeing Uncle Jack but dread spending time at Aunt Alexandra's.
- Scout and Jem feel bad that their father can't do anything interesting or impressive.
- Scout and Jem see a mad dog coming down the street, and watch as Atticus shoots it.
- Jem tells Scout not to brag to everyone that their father is a good shot, but takes a private pleasure in the fact.
- Jem buys Scout a baton, but he breaks it destroying Mrs. Dubose's camellias after the old woman insults Atticus.
- Atticus makes Jem apologize, and his punishment is to read to Mrs. Dubose every day after school.
- After her death, Mrs. Dubose's servant sends Jem a box the old woman wanted him to have.
- It contains a single camellia, and makes Jem feel like she's stalking him from beyond the grave, but Atticus tells him it's a signal that everything's all right between them.
- Jem's becoming a moody middle-schooler.
- With Atticus away on a Sunday, Calpurnia takes Scout and Jem to her own, African-American, church.
- Seeing Calpurnia at her own church prompts Scout and Jem to ask her questions about herself.
- Scout and Jem arrive home to find Aunt Alexandra on the front porch.
- When Scout finds Dill hiding under her bed, Jem tells Atticus.
- Scout and Jem watch as Atticus talks with a group of men who arrive on their doorstep one night, concerned about the Tom Robinson case.
- The next night, Jem goes out, and Scout joins him.
- Picking up Dill along the way, they go to the town square looking for Atticus.
- The trio sees him sitting in front of the jail reading, and are about to leave when some men drive up.
- While Atticus is talking to the men, Scout runs up to join them, and Jem follows with Dill.
- Atticus tells Jem to take the other two and go home, but Jem refuses.
- One of the men grabs Jem, and Scout kicks him.
- Once Scout defuses the situation, Jem walks home with Atticus, who ruffles his hair.

- The next morning, Scout, Jem, and Dill watch the crowds on the way to the courthouse for Tom's trial.
- They go to the courthouse themselves, but the only seats they can get are in the balcony where the African-Americans sit.
- Jem makes periodical whispered comments about how well the case is going for Atticus, and how it's a sure thing that Tom will be acquitted.
- After Atticus finishes his closing remarks, he finds out the kids are there, and sends them home for dinner.
- After dinner Scout, Jem, and Dill return, to find the jury still out.
- Jem is still confident that Atticus will win his case.
- When the guilty verdict comes back, Jem is heartbroken.
- The next day, Scout, Jem, and Dill try to avoid their adult neighbors, but join Miss Maudie for cake.
- After Bob Ewell spits in Atticus's face and threatens him, Scout and Jem are scared he will make good on his threats.
- After all the adults bail out of attending Scout's Halloween pageant, Jem walks Scout through the darkness to the school.
- On the way, Cecil Jacobs jumps out at Scout and Jem and scares them.
- After Scout misses her cue and feels stupid, Jem waits with her until everyone else leaves to go home.
- On their way home, Scout and Jem are attacked by someone, and Jem is knocked out.
- A stranger picks up the unconscious Jem and carries him home while Scout follows.
- Jem stays unconscious while his sister hangs out with Boo Radley, and doesn't wake up before the book ends.

Atticus Finch Character Analysis

Atticus as Father

Neither of the Finch kids ever calls their father "Dad"; he's always Atticus. While he definitely puts his foot down when necessary, he also treats his kids with respect.

For one thing, he doesn't dumb down his language to what he thinks is their level, but he also is willing to explain patiently whenever they have questions.

"I'm afraid our activities would be received with considerable disapprobation by the more learned authorities."

Jem and I were accustomed to our father's last-will-and-testament diction, and we were at all times free to interrupt Atticus for a translation when it was beyond our understanding.

"Huh, sir?"

"I never went to school," he said, "but I have a feeling that if you tell Miss Caroline we read every night she'll get after me, and I wouldn't want her after me." *(3.108-113)*

When Scout doesn't want to go back to school, Atticus doesn't just tell her that she has to go and that's that; instead, he listens to Scout's explanation of why she's upset, and tries to make her see her teacher's side of things before coming up with a compromise that makes Scout happier.

The passage above also suggests that Atticus's courtroom language creeps into the way that he talks to his kids, and so does his judicial concern with fairness. As Scout tells Uncle Jack, "When Jem an' I fuss Atticus doesn't ever just listen to Jem's side of it, he hears mine too" (9.46). Scout also tells Miss Maudie, "Atticus don't ever do anything to Jem and me in the house that he don't do in the yard" (5.53). Atticus runs his family like a judge: he's the one in charge, and has a clear set of rules that he expects his kids to follow, but he makes sure that both sides have their say.

Atticus doesn't expect his kids to respect him just because he's their father, but because he acts in a way that deserves respect. His honesty with his children means that they trust him, and look to him for guidance.

"Don't worry, Scout, it ain't time to worry yet," said Jem. He pointed. "Looka yonder."

In a group of neighbors, Atticus was standing with his hands in his overcoat pockets. He might have been watching a football game. Miss Maudie was beside him.

"See there, he's not worried yet," said Jem . (8.105-107)

Atticus is the opposite of a hypocrite: he says what he means, and lives how he thinks. In raising his children, he tries to get them to understand not only how they should behave, but why they should behave that way. This parenting attitude works most of the time, but causes problems when the kids apply Atticus's principles in ways he doesn't expect.

We were accustomed to prompt, if not always cheerful acquiescence to Atticus's instructions, but from the way he stood Jem was not thinking of budging.

"Go home, I said."

Jem shook his head. As Atticus's fists went to his hips, so did Jem's, and as they faced each other I could see little resemblance between them: Jem's soft brown hair and eyes, his oval face and snug-fitting ears were our mother's, contrasting oddly with Atticus's graying black hair and square-cut features, but they were somehow alike. Mutual defiance made them alike. (15.97-99)

Just as Atticus is standing by Tom to protect him, Jem wants to do the same for Atticus. While Atticus is not scared of the mob for his own sake, he is afraid that they'll hurt his kids. In the end, however, it's Scout's following her father's advice (talking to people about what they care about) that gets them out of their fix. While Atticus tries through his parenting to save his kids from Maycomb's intolerance, he's also giving them the same ideas that lead to him facing off with a mob and receiving death threats. Is he protecting his kids, or putting them in danger?

Perhaps the answer to both these questions is yes, because it seems that Atticus believes that shielding his kids in the short term doesn't do them any favors in the long run. This becomes especially clear when he thinks Jem is the one who stabbed Bob Ewell.

"Thank you from the bottom of my heart, but I don't want my boy starting out with something like this over his head. Best way to clear the air is to have it all out in the open. Let the county come and bring sandwiches. I don't want him growing up with a whisper about him, I don't want anybody saying, 'Jem Finch... his daddy paid a mint to get him out of that.' Sooner we get this over with the better." (30.34)

Atticus would rather his son underwent the momentary discomfort and risk of being open about his "crime" than a lifetime of second-guessing. This is, after all, the way he himself lives, doing right by Tom Robinson rather than suffer for the rest of his days the shame of having supported injustice. But does he have the right to impose the same principles on his son? Granted, he thinks it's in his son's best interest, but shouldn't Jem have a say?

While Atticus holds his children to the same high standards as he holds himself, he also is there for them when they need him. The last sentence of the novel reinforces this aspect of his character: "He turned out the light and went into Jem's room. He would be there all night, and he would be there when Jem waked up in the morning" (31.56). Even when Jem's unconscious and has no way of knowing what's going on, Atticus is there for him – because it's the right thing to do, even if no one's watching? That would fit with what we know about Atticus, but perhaps there's a simpler reason: love. (Awww.)

Atticus as Lawyer

Atticus's career as a lawyer affects his home life not just in his talking to his kids in legal jargon. His determination to defend Tom Robinson causes Jem and Scout to get a lot of grief from others in the town. Atticus tries to explain to Scout why he's doing what he's doing in this case.

"If you shouldn't be defendin' him, then why are you doin' it?"

"For a number of reasons," said Atticus. "The main one is, if I didn't I couldn't hold up my head in town, I couldn't represent this county in the legislature, I couldn't even tell you or Jem not to do something again. [...] Scout, simply by the nature of the work, every lawyer gets at least one case in his lifetime that affects him personally. This one's mine, I guess." (9.16-21)

For Atticus, being a lawyer is not just a job, it's a personal commitment to justice, and to solving problems through the law rather than through violence. There's another reason for his taking on the Tom Robinson case, however, and that's that he had no choice: Judge Taylor assigned him to the case.

"Lemme tell you somethin' now, Billy," a third said, "you know the court appointed him to

defend this nigger." "Yeah, but Atticus aims to defend him. That's what I don't like about it."

This was news, news that put a different light on things: Atticus had to, whether he wanted to or not. I thought it odd that he hadn't said anything to us about it – we could have used it many times in defending him and ourselves. He had to, that's why he was doing it, equaled fewer fights and less fussing. But did that explain the town's attitude? The court appointed Atticus to defend him. Atticus aimed to defend him. That's what they didn't like about it. It was confusing. (16.92)

Why doesn't Atticus tell Scout this, when it could have given her a good excuse to get out of fights? Perhaps because it's not really an excuse, as the quoted conversation suggests – it's not just that he's defending Tom, but that he's planning on doing it to the best of his ability, that is bothering people who think that fair trials are only for white people. Or perhaps Atticus doesn't mention it because he doesn't want Scout to defend him through the cop-out of "he's only doing it because he has to"; that may be technically true, but there's also an element of choice in how he goes about doing it.

And Atticus chooses not only to really defend Tom, rather than kinda-sorta defending him, but also to treat even the horrible Ewells with respect in court. Dill notices that Mr. Gilmer doesn't return the compliment for Tom.

"Well, Mr. Finch didn't act that way to Mayella and old man Ewell when he cross-examined them. The way that man called him 'boy' all the time an' sneered at him, an' looked around at the jury every time he answered-" (19.163)

Why the difference? Mr. Gilmer is willing to use any tools at his disposal to win his case, including taking advantage of the jury's racism. Atticus, on the other hand, appeals to the jury's sense of justice and equality. If the roles were reversed, if Atticus had been assigned the prosecution instead of the defense, would he have acted any differently? Would he have even taken the case? What part of Atticus's character does Mr. Gilmer lack, to make him able to act so differently from his legal opponent?

While Atticus's defense of Tom is consistent with what we've seen of his character up to that point, he does do something in the process that shocks even Jem and Scout.

Atticus did something I never saw him do before or since, in public or in private: he unbuttoned his vest, unbuttoned his collar, loosened his tie, and took off his coat. He never loosened a scrap of his clothing until he undressed at bedtime, and to Jem and me, this was the equivalent of him standing before us stark naked. We exchanged horrified glances.

Atticus put his hands in his pockets, and as he returned to the jury, I saw his gold collar button and the tips of his pen and pencil winking in the light.

"Gentlemen," he said. Jem and I again looked at each other: Atticus might have said, "Scout." His voice had lost its aridity, its detachment, and he was talking to the jury as if they were folks on the post office corner. (20.38-40)

Why this sudden informality? Perhaps this is Atticus's version of a presidential candidate donning a flannel shirt to connect with the common man. Or perhaps he's trying to suggest that he's speaking honestly, not as a lawyer trying to get his client off, but as one man to another. Or perhaps it's just really, really hot in the courtroom. The end of his closing remarks, however, suggests that it has something to do with awakening the jury's humanity.

"I'm no idealist to believe firmly in the integrity of our courts and in the jury system – that is no ideal to me, it is a living, working reality. Gentlemen, a court is no better than each man of you sitting before me on this jury. A court is only as sound as its jury, and a jury is only as sound as the men who make it up. I am confident that you gentlemen will review without passion the evidence you have heard, come to a decision, and restore this defendant to his family. In the name of God, do your duty." (20.52)

For Atticus, Tom's trial means more than the fate of a single man, though all signs do point to his caring about Tom as an individual. It even means more than a referendum on racism in Maycomb. From a broader perspective, the case is about the fairness of the American legal system, which means it's about the fairness of American people. In his closing remarks, Atticus argues for big principles like equality and duty, but he doesn't for a moment lose sight of the fact that in the end it's human beings and their choices that make equality stand or fall – in this case, fall.

Atticus Finch Timeline and Summary

- Atticus grows up in Finches' Landing, but leaves to go to law school.
- After being admitted to the bar, Atticus sets up shop in Maycomb, twenty miles from where he grew up, where he's related to nearly everyone.
- With his first lawyerly earnings he puts his younger brother through medical school.
- After joining the state legislature, Atticus marries a woman fifteen years younger than him, and has two kids with her before she dies.
- After Calpurnia chews Scout out for being rude to Walter Cunningham, Scout tells Atticus to get rid of her, but Atticus tells her to do what Calpurnia tells her.
- When Scout comes home depressed because her teacher says she can't read with Atticus anymore, Atticus tells her they can still do so long as she doesn't tell the teacher.
- When Atticus sees the kids playing the Radley game, he doesn't tell them to stop, but he makes his disapproval clear.
- Atticus catches Jem and Dill trying to give a note to Boo Radley, and uses lawyer tricks to get Jem to admit what they were doing.
- On the night of Maycomb's first snowfall in years, Atticus wakes up his kids because Miss Maudie's house is on fire.
- Before the flames get too bad, Atticus saves Miss Maudie's most prized possession, a rocking chair.
- When it's clear the house is lost, Atticus stands back and lets the firefighters do their job, and tells his kids that they don't need to worry about their own house yet but they should stay out of the way by the Radley Place.

- When the fire is out and they return to their house, Atticus at first thinks the kids disobeyed him because of Scout's new blanket, but soon figures out that it must have been Boo.
- Scout asks Atticus about the Tom Robinson case, and Atticus explains his position to her.
- At Christmas, Atticus takes Scout home from Aunt Alexandra's in disgrace after she fights with her cousin Francis.
- Atticus talks to Uncle Jack about the Robinson case, knowing that Scout is listening from around the corner.
- Atticus refuses to teach his kids how to use their new air rifles, but only tells them not to shoot at mockingbirds.
- The kids are ashamed when Atticus refuses to join in on the football game that a town church is having for a fundraiser.
- Calpurnia calls Atticus to tell him about the mad dog in their street, and he brings Sheriff Tate over to kill the dog.
- It's a difficult shot, so Tate insists that Atticus take it, even though he protests.
- Atticus kills the dog with one bullet.
- When Jem takes out his anger at mean Mrs. Dubose by destroying her camellias, Atticus not only makes him go back and apologize, he also makes him do as Mrs. Dubose wishes and read to her every afternoon.
- After Mrs. Dubose dies, Atticus tells the kids that she was a morphine addict trying to get clean before she died, and talks about her courage.
- Atticus returns from the state capital to explain to the kids why Aunt Alexandra has come to live with them.
- Aunt Alexandra tries to get Atticus to talk to the kids about their family pride, but all he can do is make Scout cry so he gives up on it, and makes Aunt Alexandra drop it too.
- Scout asks Atticus what rape is, and he tells her.
- Atticus makes Scout obey her Aunt Alexandra, even though her views on what Scout should and shouldn't do are different from his.
- Atticus defends Calpurnia when Aunt Alexandra wants to get rid of her.
- When the kids find Dill under Scout's bed, Atticus talks to his family and arranges for him to stay.
- One night a group of men come to talk to Atticus about their fears concerning the Tom Robinson case.
- The next night, Atticus camps out in front of the jail where Tom is being held.
- When the kids turn up, Atticus is afraid for their safety, but ultimately he is relieved that they kept the situation from turning ugly.
- Atticus goes to court to defend Tom Robinson.
- Atticus gets Tate to give him the facts that he needs, manages not to laugh at the absurd (though dangerous) Bob Ewell, reluctantly attacks Mayella in order to try to save his client, and lets Tom tell his story in his own words.
- In his closing remarks, he not only talks about the case itself, but about the wider racial prejudice that is the main reason the case wasn't dismissed for lack of evidence before it ever came to trial.
- After the guilty verdict, Atticus leaves the courtroom alone, and the African-Americans in the balcony stand up to honor him.
- After the trial, Atticus is bitter, but he hopes to win the case on appeal.
- Bob Ewell is also bitter, threatening Atticus in public and spitting in his face.
- Atticus tells the kids that the only person on the jury willing to acquit Tom was a relative of

the Mr. Cunningham Scout had faced down in the lynch mob.
- One day Atticus comes home in the middle of one of Aunt Alexandra's tea parties with bad news: Tom has been shot and killed while trying to escape from prison.
- Atticus takes Calpurnia and goes to break the news to Helen Robinson, Tom's wife.
- Atticus is too tired (or so he says) to attend Scout's Halloween pageant.
- When Jem is carried in unconscious, Atticus first tends to him, then calls Heck Tate.
- Atticus at first wants Jem to undergo legal proceedings for stabbing Ewell because he doesn't want it to seem like he's covering anything up, but Heck Tate convinces him that whatever happened, taking the case to court would mean publicity for Boo, which would be a sin.
- Atticus worries that Scout won't understand, but she does.
- After Scout walks Boo home, Atticus reads to her at her request until she falls asleep.
- Atticus stays with the sleeping Jem all night, until he wakes up in the morning.

Calpurnia Character Analysis

Calpurnia's Tough Love

While everyone in the novel is filtered through Scout's perception – she is, after all, the narrator – Calpurnia in particular appears for a long time more as Scout's idea of her than as a real person. At the beginning of the novel, Scout thinks of Calpurnia as the wicked stepmother to Scout's own Cinderella.

She was all angles and bones; she was nearsighted; she squinted; her hand was wide as a bed slat and twice as hard. She was always ordering me out of the kitchen, asking me why I couldn't behave as well as Jem when she knew he was older, and calling me home when I wasn't ready to come. Our battles were epic and one-sided. Calpurnia always won, mainly because Atticus always took her side. She had been with us ever since Jem was born, and I had felt her tyrannical presence as long as I could remember. (1.12)

Scout at first sees Calpurnia less as a human being than as a force of nature that she runs up against all too often. Scout thinks Calpurnia wins their battles not because she has right on her side, but because she has the might, and that for her to be kind would be to admit defeat.

Calpurnia bent down and kissed me. I ran along, wondering what had come over her. She had wanted to make up with me, that was it. She had always been too hard on me, she had at last seen the error of her fractious ways, she was sorry and too stubborn to say so. (3.75)

Caught up in the tunnel vision of her own perspective, Scout can't see that Calpurnia is hard on her because she cares about her.

Calpurnia's Double Life

By taking the Finch kids with her to First Purchase Church, Calpurnia shows them a different side of her character. In this new setting of Maycomb's African-American community, Calpurnia surprises Jem and Scout by speaking in a voice they'd never heard her use before.

"Cal," I asked, "why do you talk nigger-talk to the – to your folks when you know it's not right?"

[…] "Suppose you and Scout talked colored-folks' talk at home it'd be out of place, wouldn't it? Now what if I talked white-folks' talk at church, and with my neighbors? They'd think I was puttin' on airs to beat Moses."

"But Cal, you know better," I said.

"It's not necessary to tell all you know. It's not ladylike – in the second place, folks don't like to have somebody around knowin' more than they do. It aggravates 'em. You're not gonna change any of them by talkin' right, they've got to want to learn themselves, and when they don't want to learn there's nothing you can do but keep your mouth shut or talk their language." (12.139-144)

Calpurnia teaches Scout and Jem about community values, and their relativity: what's right in one place may be wrong in another. But is that always true? Atticus is famous for acting the same everywhere, and that's presented as a good thing. Why can Atticus always be the same, while Calpurnia has to adapt herself depending on the community she's in? Is one of these approaches more successful than the other?

Seeing Calpurnia in relation to the African-American community causes Scout to realize for the first time that Cal actually continues to exist when she's not at the Finch house.

That Calpurnia led a modest double life never dawned on me. The idea that she had a separate existence outside our household was a novel one, to say nothing of her having command of two languages. (12.138)

This revelation sparks Scout's curiosity about Calpurnia, and she peppers her with basic questions like when her birthday is (she doesn't actually know, not even the year) and where she grew up (near Finches' Landing). While Cal shares the basic facts of her life, what isn't revealed is her feelings about them. Does she miss her childhood home? Was she happy there? Did she leave family members behind? What does she do on her days off? While Scout does learn to see Calpurnia as a real person over the course of the novel, the question remains open of to what extent the novel gives Calpurnia an identity separate from her role as the Finch kids' Giver of Life Lessons.

Charles Baker Harris (Dill) Character Analysis

For Scout and Jem, summer means Dill, and Dill's imagination: "Thus we came to know Dill as a pocket Merlin, whose head teemed with eccentric plans, strange longings, and quaint fancies"

(1.39). While the Finch kids, despite their imaginative flights of fancy, are firmly entrenched in the reality of Maycomb, Dill's outsider status causes him to see the Maycomb community from a different perspective.

This becomes most clear at Tom Robinson's trial. While Scout accepts Mr. Gilmer's rude treatment of Tom on the witness stand as normal, Dill starts crying uncontrollably at the injustice of Tom's being treated so differently from the white witnesses. He can't quite explain his feelings, but Mr. Raymond can.

"Things haven't caught up with that one's instinct yet. Let him get a little older and he won't get sick and cry [...] about the simple hell people give other people – without even thinking. Cry about the hell white people give colored folks, without even stopping to think that they're people, too." (20.20-22)

Dill's sensitivity to Maycomb's intolerance gives Scout, and the reader, a different model of how to respond to what's happening. The contrast between Dill's angry tears and Scout's justification of Mr. Gilmer's attitude with the surprisingly callous "he's just a Negro" (19.164) suggests that Scout's already been hit with Maycomb's ugly racism stick – that neither being a child nor being Atticus's daughter has been enough to shield her entirely from her community's prejudices. Or maybe she's just trying to comfort Dill.

While Scout and Jem struggle after the trial to make sense of the Maycomb community that they thought they knew so well, and to figure out their own place in it, Dill's outsider status allows him to take a more detached approach.

"I think I'll be a clown when I get grown [...] There ain't one thing in this world I can do about folks except laugh, so I'm gonna join the circus and laugh my head off."

"You got it backwards, Dill," said Jem. "Clowns are sad, it's folks that laugh at them."

"Well I'm gonna be a new kind of clown. I'm gonna stand in the middle of the ring and laugh at the folks." (22.60-64)

While Mr. Raymond predicts that Dill will grow out of crying into not caring, Dill himself comes up with a different path, hiding the tears in laughter. Both responses, however, are difficult for Scout to understand. Dill's character suggests what the limitations of Scout's perspective might be, giving the reader a broader picture of what's the matter with Maycomb through the different limitations of Dill's viewpoint.

Arthur Radley (Boo) Character Analysis

Boo the Monster

Boo first comes into the novel through the creative imagination of Jem, whose description of his neighbor suggests that if he had been born several decades later, he would probably be shooting homemade zombie movies on digital video in his backyard.

Jem gave a reasonable description of Boo: Boo was about six-and-a-half feet tall, judging from his tracks; he dined on raw squirrels and any cats he could catch, that's why his hands were bloodstained – if you ate an animal raw, you could never wash the blood off. There was a long jagged scar that ran across his face; what teeth he had were yellow and rotten; his eyes popped, and he drooled most of the time. (1.65)

Talking about Boo gives kids the same thrill as telling scary stories around a campfire. Never having seen him, they don't quite believe he is a real person, and so they're free to make up fantastic stories as someone else might do about Bigfoot. Their make-believe games, in which they act out scenes from his life, put him on the same level as the horror novels they shiver over. Are they really interested in Boo, or does he just serve as a convenient excuse for fun games to lighten up a boring summer? Perhaps the answer is different for different combinations of the kids at different times.

Boo the Fantasy

While Boo can be a figure of fear, there's also a strange longing for connection in the kids' obsession with him. Their acting out of the life and times of Boo Radley could, after all, be seen as a way to try to understand him by trying on his skin, as Atticus always says. And at least some of their attempts to see him they explain as concern for his well-being.

Dill said, "We're askin' him real politely to come out sometimes, and tell us what he does in there – we said we wouldn't hurt him and we'd buy him an ice cream."

"You all've gone crazy, he'll kill us!"

Dill said, "It's my idea. I figure if he'd come out and sit a spell with us he might feel better."

"How do you know he don't feel good?"

"Well how'd you feel if you'd been shut up for a hundred years with nothin' but cats to eat?" (5.72-76)

The last line suggests that Dill at least feels some sympathy for Boo, and can imagine, or thinks he can imagine what he feels – and what he needs. Why are they so bent on making him come out? Perhaps Boo becomes such a figure of fascination for the kids because he makes them ask the question: can you still be human without being part of a community? Meeting Boo might answer this question, and also fill in the gaping hole that the Radley Place forms in Maycomb's social world.

Boo the Reality

After the Tom Robinson trial, Jem and Scout start to have a different understanding of Boo Radley.

"Scout, I think I'm beginning to understand something. I think I'm beginning to understand why

Boo Radley's stayed shut up in the house all this time... it's because he wants to stay inside." (23.117)

Having seen a sample of the horrible things their fellow townspeople can do, choosing to stay out of the mess of humanity doesn't seem like such a strange choice.

When Boo finally does come out, he has a good reason: Bob Ewell is trying to murder the Finch kids. No one sees what happens in the scuffle, but at the end of it, Ewell is dead and Boo is carrying an unconscious Jem to the Finch house. Finally faced with Boo, Scout doesn't even recognize him: after all, she's never seen him before, except in her dreams.

While Tate insists that Ewell fell on his own knife, he also indirectly implies that Boo stabbed the man on purpose to defend the children. Since no one saw it (except, presumably, Boo), there's no way to know for certain. Rather than drag Boo into court, Tate decides to "let the dead bury their dead" (30.60). However, Tate seems less concerned about the negative consequences for Boo than the positive ones.

"Know what'd happen then? All the ladies in Maycomb includin' my wife'd be knocking on his door bringing angel food cakes. To my way of thinkin', Mr. Finch, taking the one man who's done you and this town a great service an' draggin' him with his shy ways into the limelight – to me, that's a sin. It's a sin and I'm not about to have it on my head. If it was any other man, it'd be different. But not this man, Mr. Finch." (30.62)

Oh no, angel food cakes! Spare him the horror! But for Boo, being the center of attention, even good attention, would be horrible. Even Scout, who's known the real Boo for less than an hour, gets it: "Well, it'd be sort of like shootin' a mockingbird, wouldn't it?" (30.68). Boo causes even the total-equality-under-the-law Atticus to think that sometimes a little inequality is what's really fair.

When Scout walks Boo home, she's entering into territory she's seen all her life but never before set foot on. Turning to leave, she sees her familiar neighborhood from a new perspective – Boo's perspective.

To the left of the brown door was a long shuttered window. I walked to it, stood in front of it, and turned around. In daylight, I thought, you could see to the postoffice corner. [...]

Fall, and his children trotted to and fro around the corner, the day's woes and triumphs on their faces. They stopped at an oak tree, delighted, puzzled, apprehensive.

Winter, and his children shivered at the front gate, silhouetted against a blazing house. [...]

Summer, and he watched his children's heart break. Autumn again, and Boo's children needed him.

Atticus was right. One time he said you never really know a man until you stand in his shoes and walk around in them. Just standing on the Radley porch was enough. (31.25-31)

Boo transforms from an evil spirit into a guardian angel just through a shift in perspective. And, while meeting Boo in person is part of what spurs this change, what really cements it for Scout is an act of imagination, as she visualizes what the events of the last few years might have looked like to Boo. This turn of events suggests that in order to understand and sympathize with others, all you need is imagination. Perhaps that's one reason why children are held up throughout the novel as being less subject to the prejudices of their elders – they make better use of their imaginations. Imagining Boo as a monster had little in common with reality, but it did get the kids in the habit of trying to figure out how Boo sees the world.

The book ends with a sleepy Scout retelling the story Atticus has just been reading to her.

"An' they chased him 'n' never could catch him 'cause they didn't know what he looked like, an' Atticus, when they finally saw him, why he hadn't done any of those things... Atticus, he was real nice...." His hands were under my chin, pulling up the cover, tucking it around me.

"Most people are, Scout, when you finally see them." (31.55)

Scout literally "finally sees" Boo, but perhaps there's more to "seeing" than that. The Tom Robinson case suggests that it's all too possible for people to look at someone and still not see that he's a human being just like them.

Boo starts out a monster and ends up a man, but he never rejoins the Maycomb community. Or perhaps, in taking an active interest in the Finch children, he already has: perhaps his character suggests that the bonds that hold a community together can be more than just social ones.

Thomas Robinson Character Analysis

Before the Trial: Invisible Man

Like Boo Radley, the character of Tom Robinson has an existence in the imagination of Maycomb that extends far beyond himself as an individual. On one level, Tom is a human being caught up and destroyed by Maycomb's racism, but he also serves as a litmus test for the consciences of the whites of Maycomb.

The name of Tom Robinson comes up long before he appears in person. The main issue setting tongues wagging is not, however, whether Tom is innocent or guilty, but rather Atticus's resolve to give him a good defense. Tom himself is virtually absent from these debates, which assume either that he's guilty or that, regardless of his guilt or innocence, he should be punished for getting anywhere near Mayella.

Tom's invisibility continues even through his first appearance in the novel. When the lynch mob turns up at the jail where he's being held, they face off with Atticus while Tom himself listens silently from inside. It's not until after they leave that Tom's disembodied voice comes out of the darkness.

"Mr. Finch?"

A soft husky voice came from the darkness above: "They gone?"

Atticus stepped back and looked up. "They've gone," he said. "Get some sleep, Tom. They won't bother you any more." (15.128-130)

The conflict is between white people, with Tom as the unseen, powerless object they're fighting over. So why don't we see Tom until the day of the trial? The obvious answer is that we don't because Scout doesn't – but the novel could have brought Tom and Scout together at some point, so why didn't it? One answer is that if she had seen him, we wouldn't have the big reveal at the trial of Tom's disability, while doing things this way allows us to wonder along with the rest of the audience why Atticus is making such a big deal of Ewell's left-handedness.

But there might be more going on here: how real a person does Tom seem before we see him? And how sympathetic does he seem? Getting an idea of Tom only through what people say about him puts us as readers in a similar position to the people of Maycomb in terms of how much knowledge we have about him, but it's up to us to make up our own minds about Tom – and about the people who judge him.

At the Trial: Tom the Beast vs. Tom the Man

Even when Tom appears in person for the first time at the trial, everyone else gets to give their version of what happened before he has a chance to speak. At the trial, we get two versions of his relationship with Mayella, and they offer two very different stories: Mayella and her father tell the story that everyone expects to hear, about the Tom that is the town's nightmare, and Tom tells the story that no one wants to hear, about the Tom that is himself.

The Ewells' Tom is a wicked beast who acts out of animalistic lust. Neither father nor daughter gives a motivation for his sudden attack on Mayella – it seems assumed that of course any African-American man would rape any white woman, given the chance. (Atticus points out the faultiness of this assumption in his closing remarks; see "Race" in "Quotes and Thoughts" for more.) The Ewells' Tom draws both on white fears of African-American men, especially where white women are concerned, and also on the stereotypes that justify white oppression of supposedly inferior African-Americans.

As Tom presents himself, however, he's a good guy who was just trying to help out a fellow human being in need. The only feelings he has for Mayella are compassion and pity, but it seems even those aren't acceptable either.

"You're a mighty good fellow, it seems – did all this for not one penny?"

"Yes, suh. I felt right sorry for her, she seemed to try more'n the rest of 'em-"

*"*You *felt sorry for* her, *you felt* sorry *for her?" Mr. Gilmer seemed ready to rise to the ceiling.*

The witness realized his mistake and shifted uncomfortably in the chair. But the damage was done. Below us, nobody liked Tom Robinson's answer. Mr. Gilmer paused a long time to let it sink in. (19.124-127)

Tom feels sorry for Mayella as one human being for another, but Mr. Gilmer and others can only see a black man feeling sorry for a white woman, suggesting the uncomfortable-for-them idea that white skin doesn't make a person automatically better off than anyone whose skin is black.

In his testimony, Tom presents himself as someone caught in an impossible situation: Mayella's behavior, as Atticus says, breaks the code of acceptable black-white relations, and so there's no right way for Tom to respond.

"Mr. Finch, I tried. I tried to 'thout bein' ugly to her. I didn't wanta be ugly, I didn't wanta push her or nothin'."[...]

Until my father explained it to me later, I did not understand the subtlety of Tom's predicament: he would not have dared strike a white woman under any circumstances and expect to live long, so he took the first opportunity to run – a sure sign of guilt. (19.76-77)

Tom does the best he can under the circumstances, but even his best is not good enough, since so few people want to think the best of him.

The Verdict: No Chance

Faced with two stories, one comfortable (even if it is about rape) and familiar, the other disturbing and challenging, the jury has a choice of which one to believe (or at least to say they believe). And, as Atticus tells Scout earlier, "this case [...] is something that goes to the essence of a man's conscience" (11.53). As a character, Tom serves as a litmus test to divide Maycomb into those who put facts above fears and prejudice, and those who put their beliefs as to the way the world works over what the evidence actually suggests is true.

While everyone in Maycomb faces this same choice, it's the jury alone whose verdict will decide Tom's fate. The decision the jury faces is not, however, whether Tom is innocent or guilty, but simply whether the prosecution has presented enough evidence to prove Tom's guilt beyond a shadow of a doubt. Atticus says no, Jem strongly agrees, but in the end, the jury does not.

Does the jury actually think Tom raped Mayella, or are they just afraid to say otherwise? Without a fly-on-the-wall narrator in the jury room, it's hard to tell. We do know that the one jury member who was willing to acquit Tom was a relative of Mr. Cunningham, who was part of the mob that tried to lynch Tom. What made this unknown Cunningham's views on Tom different? He didn't have access to any additional evidence, but he did have a connection with someone who felt sympathy with the defense – perhaps that was enough to ignite a spark of bravery to go against accepted opinion and acquit Tom. Or perhaps he was inspired by Atticus's determined stand for what he believed in to do the same.

Aftermath: No Hope

After the guilty verdict that ignores Tom's own version of himself in favor of Maycomb's nightmare vision of him, Tom loses hope (and again disappears from the narrative). Atticus promises him an appeal, but who's to say the white men at the next level up will be any different than the fine citizens of Maycomb? Tom's escape attempt seems crazy – running across a football-field sized prison yard to climb a fence in broad daylight with several armed guards watching – but perhaps that's the only way he saw of taking control of his fate. As Atticus says afterwards, "I guess Tom was tired of white men's chances and preferred to take his own" (24.71). Or perhaps Tom just couldn't take it any more and snapped, like Jem and Mrs. Dubose's camellia bushes.

In any case, Tom's death changes little about how Maycomb sees him, and in fact just reinforces their stereotypes further.

To Maycomb, Tom's death was typical. Typical of a nigger to cut and run. Typical of a nigger's mentality to have no plan, no thought for the future, just run blind first chance he saw. Funny thing, Atticus Finch might've got him off scot free, but wait-? Hell no. You know how they are. Easy come, easy go. Just shows you, that Robinson boy was legally married, they say he kept himself clean, went to church and all that, but when it comes down to the line the veneer's mighty thin. Nigger always comes out in 'em. (25.25)

Just like Tom's running away from the Ewell house gives most of Maycomb another excuse to believe in his guilt, his running away from prison once again gets worked into their pre-existing ideas about what African-Americans are like. And just as no amount of white blood can overcome a drop of black blood in Maycomb genetics, no amount of good behavior can save Tom from condemnation for any act that can possibly be perceived as bad. What's more, it's not just Tom personally who is condemned for his faults, but the entire African-American race. That's one way stereotypes work. (Here's a comic strip with a quick-n-easy illustration of this thought process.)

While Atticus takes pride in getting Tom the fairest trial possible under the circumstances, and takes some hope in the fact that the jury took hours instead of minutes to reach the foregone conclusion of a guilty verdict, Mr. Underwood's postmortem newspaper editorial sees the whole trial as a sham.

"Atticus had used every tool available to free men to save Tom Robinson, but in the secret courts of men's hearts Atticus had no case. Tom was a dead man the minute Mayella Ewell opened her mouth and screamed." (25.28)

If it's true that in Tom's personal Choose-Your-Own-Adventure all paths lead to conviction, the question arises: what in Maycomb would have to change for Tom to have the chance of a different fate? What would have to change for him to be able to control that fate? And what does Tom's fate as it stands say about Maycomb as a community?

Mayella Violet Ewell Character Analysis

Among the trash and cast-offs in the Ewell yard, there's one spot of beauty.

"Against the fence, in a line, were six chipped-enamel slop jars holding brilliant red geraniums, cared for as tenderly as if they belonged to Miss Maudie Atkinson, had Miss Maudie deigned to permit a geranium on her premises. People said they were Mayella Ewell's." (17.64)

The geraniums suggest that Mayella desires to be better than her surroundings, to make something bright in her dull world, to aspire to higher things. But whatever Mayella's hopes and dreams are, she doesn't get a chance to express them to the reader; she appears only at Tom's trial, where she's performing a role for public consumption, that of the poor innocent white woman attacked by the evil black man, who must be protected by chivalrous white men.

Throughout the book there's a tension between what Mayella is (a Ewell) and what she needs to be to justify the condemnation of Tom Robinson (the flower of "Southern womanhood," an idea that itself is, according to Atticus, a "polite fiction" [15.39]).

"A young girl walked to the witness stand. As she raised her hand and swore that the evidence she gave would be the truth, the whole truth, and nothing but the truth so help her God, she seemed somehow fragile-looking, but when she sat facing us in the witness chair she became what she was, a thick-bodied girl accustomed to strenuous labor." (18.2)

In order to convict Tom, the jury has to believe in, or at least pretend to believe in, the fragile, helpless girl who gets taken advantage of by Tom, rather than the desperate, lonely woman who actively desires him. It's not just ideals of what women are that's at stake, but also of men, as Mayella's challenge to the court makes clear.

"I got somethin' to say an' then I ain't gonna say no more. That nigger yonder took advantage of me an' if you fine fancy gentlemen don't wanta do nothin' about it then you're all yellow stinkin' cowards, stinkin' cowards, the lot of you. Your fancy airs don't come to nothin' – your ma'amin' and Miss Mayellerin' don't come to nothin', Mr. Finch-" Then she burst into real tears.(18.167)

Mayella's comment suggests that for men to be big brave heroes, they have to believe that women are helpless timid victims in need of protection or avenging. According to this logic, proper men have to take Mayella's word over Tom's, or risk having their Man Licenses revoked, because Man has been defined as He Who Protects Women, not as He Who Listens Carefully To All The Evidence And Makes A Rational, Considered Judgment Based On The Facts.

Despite Mayella's trash status as a Ewell, in accusing a black man she's able to access the privileges of white Southern womanhood – namely, the chivalrous protection of men, no questions asked. If she had told Heck Tate that it was her father who beat her up, would she be in court testifying against him? Perhaps, but there certainly wouldn't be the huge audience that turns out to see Tom convicted. The difference between this imaginary case and the one that happens in the novel suggests that the way characters think about race and the way they think about gender are intertwined – the Tom Robinson case isn't just about race, or just about gender, but about the intersection of the two.

Why doesn't Mayella tell the truth about what happened? One reason is probably that she's scared of her father, who the evidence suggests has beaten and perhaps even sexually abused her in the past. Atticus gives another reason in his closing remarks: guilt at doing an "unspeakable" thing, "kiss[ing] a black man" (20.45).

"She did something every child has done – she tried to put the evidence of her offense away from her. But in this case she was no child hiding stolen contraband: she struck out at her victim – of necessity she must put him away from her – he must be removed from her presence, from this world. She must destroy the evidence of her offense."What was the evidence of her offense? Tom Robinson, a human being." (20-43-44)

In comparing Mayella to a child, Atticus brings together the two opposite ideas of womanhood: yes, he's saying, she's naïve and weak (which is almost, but not quite, the same thing as innocent and helpless), but she also feels guilty because of her desire for Tom, which is causing her to commit the crime of perjury. If we agree with Atticus's version of her character, which seems reasonable based on what we've seen first-hand of her testimony in court (though of course, everything is filtered through Scout's perspective; see "Narrator Point of View" for more on this), Mayella is dealing with her own self-hatred for having a desire that society tells her is wrong by saying that she's not the one with the desire, Tom is, and by destroying him the desire is destroyed. Or perhaps she doesn't see anything wrong with what she did, just that she got caught, and is now trying to do damage control with her father by saying whatever he wants her to say.

In any case, after Tom's conviction Mayella goes back to her flowers on the trash heap, and Maycomb stops caring about her. She never reappears in the novel, but perhaps her father's death will give her the opportunity to make good on the promise of geraniums.

Robert E. Lee Ewell Character Analysis

Bob Ewell is the current head of a family that has been "the disgrace of Maycomb for three generations" (3.93). Considered human trash by the Maycomb community, the Ewells live in a shotgun shack out by the dump. Ewell has no ambition to improve his life, or the lives of his eight motherless children; instead, he spends his welfare checks on whiskey and has the local landowners turn a blind eye to his poaching activities out of pity for his hungry children.

On the one hand, Bob seems an object of pity in that he was doomed from the moment he was born an Ewell, but on the other, he's such an obnoxious and mean character that it's hard to feel sorry for him. While the town's view that he's just an Ewell, and Ewells are trash, is their way of making sense of his behavior, it also makes it easy for the town to avoid responsibility for trying to help him or his children: no point in offering any aid to someone who's not going to change.

Scout first sees Mr. Ewell at Tom Robinson's trial. She thinks he looks like a freshly-scrubbed rooster, and he's about as articulate as a dirty-minded Foghorn Leghorn. On the witness stand, he plays the comedian even with the lawyer for his own side.

Mr. Ewell was Mr. Gilmer's witness, and he had no business being rude to him of all people.

"Are you the father of Mayella Ewell?" was the next question.

"Well, if I ain't I can't do nothing about it now, her ma's dead," was the answer. (17.70-72)

It seems that Mr. Ewell's default position is to be antagonistic to everyone, even people who are supposed to be on his own side; no wonder he has no friends. His response is not only a rude attempt to impress others by making a joke, it also hints at how Ewell sees women in general: lying cheating whores whose deaths are to be laughed about. From his first words, Ewell shows that respect for others is as foreign to him as personal hygiene, and his later testimony does nothing to change that impression. His statement of Tom's supposed crime is couched in the most offensive terms possible, calculated to stir up people's emotions and fears to evidence-ignoring levels of irrationality. (See "Race" in "Quotes and Thoughts" for more on Ewell's accusation of Tom.)

After the trial, Ewell isn't satisfied to have gotten Tom sentenced to death; he wants revenge on those that would give him a fair trial. It's likely that Ewell is the shadow Judge Taylor sees at his house one night, but it's Atticus and Helen that get the brunt of his rage. Atticus doesn't say much about his confrontation with Ewell, so his kids get the Miss-Stephanie-enhanced version: "Atticus was leaving the post office when Mr. Ewell approached him, cursed him, spat on him, and threatened to kill him" (23.2).

While the Maycomb community is happy enough to return to ignoring the Ewells after their day in court, Ewell won't go quietly back to the dump, but instead wants to assert his power through threats of violence to anyone associated in his mind with Tom Robinson. It's as if what Tom did in Ewell's mind is so horrible that destroying Tom himself isn't enough – Ewell has to wipe out all traces of him. Or perhaps it's just revenge – after all, Scout and Jem don't have much to do with Tom directly, but attacking them is a powerful way to hurt Atticus.

If we believe Tom's testimony that Mayella approached him, and that Ewell's anger was directed first at her rather than Tom, why is Ewell so determined to prosecute Tom and persecute those involved with him? A comment of Scout's offers one key to unlock this question: "All the little man on the witness stand had that made him any better than his nearest neighbors was, that if scrubbed with lye soap in very hot water, his skin was white" (17.67).

Ewell's "nearest neighbors" are African-Americans, so racism (and, if we recall his first answer on the witness stand, sexism) is the only way that Ewell can feel superior to anybody. There's not a single white man in Maycomb who's not above Ewell in the community hierarchy, so perhaps he turns with all the more venom on those he thinks he can put below him: African-Americans and women. What would it take for Ewell to overcome his background and become a more tolerant person? Short of a miracle, it's hard to say.

Alexandra Hancock Character Analysis

Aunt Alexandra is so different from her easy-going brothers Atticus and Jack that Scout wonders if she was switched at birth with another family's baby. She's the kind of woman who wears a corset even under her bathrobe. Scout compares her to Mount Everest: "throughout my early life, she was cold and there" (9.36). And whenever Scout expresses a desire to do something Aunty believes is Not Done By Finches, she's down on her niece like an avalanche.

She had said Indeed Not, but this time she would give her reasons: "But I want to play with Walter, Aunty, why can't I?"

She took off her glasses and stared at me. "I'll tell you why," she said. "Because – he – is – trash, that's why you can't play with him. I'll not have you around him, picking up his habits and learning Lord-knows-what." (23.86-87)

Aunty sees the Finch name like an exclusive brand – it's valuable when you can only find it at Bloomingdale's, but make it available at Wal-Mart and it'll seem cheap. Aunt Alexandra's obsession with "What Is Best For the Family" (13.22) – in Scout's ears, Aunty often speaks in Capital Letters Of Doom – is part of her more general way of classifying people by family heritage.

Aunt Alexandra, in underlining the moral of young Sam Merriweather's suicide, said it was caused by a morbid streak in the family. Let a sixteen-year-old girl giggle in the choir and Aunty would say, "It just goes to show you, all the Penfield women are flighty." Everybody in Maycomb, it seemed, had a Streak: a Drinking Streak, a Gambling Streak, a Mean Streak, a Funny Streak. (13.26)

Her obsession with Family Streaks suggests an underlying belief that Family is Destiny – and that Finches are Destined to be superior. But she uses that Destiny as a metaphorical club to beat Scout into line with – the Finch Grand Destiny apparently only holds true so long as Finch family members Live Up To It, and Scout's lack of concern for the Dignity of her Heritage could damage the Family Standing. (Looks like Capital Letters Of Doom are Contagious.)

Besides instilling the Finch kids with a sense of their own importance in being Finches, Aunt Alexandra's other mission is to make sure Scout grows up into a nice young lady. She sets to work trying to quash Scout's tomboyish tendencies and to prepare her for a life of docile domesticity.

Aunt Alexandra was fanatical on the subject of my attire. I could not possibly hope to be a lady if I wore breeches; when I said I could do nothing in a dress, she said I wasn't supposed to be doing things that required pants. Aunt Alexandra's vision of my deportment involved playing with small stoves, tea sets, and wearing the Add-A-Pearl necklace she gave me when I was born; furthermore, I should be a ray of sunshine in my father's lonely life. (9.74)

Scout, however, would much rather get dirty, swear, and shoot her air rifle with her older brother Jem. Scout holds out against her aunt's attempts to convert her into a dreaded girl, but is also strangely fascinated by her aunt's mysterious world of ladies' tea parties, which seem to operate according to an entirely different set of rules. At the tea party where Miss Maudie takes down Mrs. Merriweather for talking smack about the Robinson case, one moment in particular mystifies Scout.

When she had them well on the road with Mrs. Perkins, Aunt Alexandra stepped back. She gave Miss Maudie a look of pure gratitude, and I wondered at the world of women. Miss Maudie and Aunt Alexandra had never been especially close, and here was Aunty silently thanking her for something. For what, I knew not. I was content to learn that Aunt Alexandra could be pierced sufficiently to feel gratitude for help given. (24.53)

It's unclear whether recent experiences have caused Aunt Alexandra to thaw slightly, or if it's Scout who has started seeing her more clearly, just as it takes a change of scene for Scout to see Calpurnia as a full person. In any case, it seems Aunt Alexandra's direct lessons to Scout on How To Be A Lady have less of an effect on her niece's ascent into ladyhood than Scout's observation of these fleeting moments when Aunt Alexandra demonstrates by example what being a lady means.

Ironically, Aunt Alexandra's concern for Family causes her to go head to head with her brother Atticus, whose defense of Tom Robinson, Aunt Alexandra thinks, might endanger the Finch reputation. In the end, however, it's family affection that looms largest for Aunt Alexandra. After Tom is shot trying to escape, Alexandra tells Miss Maudie, "I can't say I approve of everything he does, Maudie, but he's my brother, and I just want to know when this will ever end. [...] It tears him to pieces" (24.76). While Aunt Alexandra is the voice of a particular kind of family values throughout the novel, she also stands by her family when they need her – though it's uncertain whether that's because of her values or in spite of them.

Maudie Atkinson Character Analysis

Miss Maudie is part of the world where "fragrant ladies rocked slowly, fanned gently, and drank cool water" (24.53) that Scout both desires and fears, but this rose never lets others forget her thorns. Unlike Miss Stephanie and Mrs. Dubose, however, Miss Maudie uses her sharp tongue to counter meanness rather than to perpetrate it. When Miss Stephanie tries to spread tales of Boo's fearsomeness, Miss Maudie doesn't just refuse to listen, or even just smile and nod and forget.

"Stephanie Crawford even told me once she woke up in the middle of the night and found him looking in the window at her. I said what did you do, Stephanie, move over in the bed and make room for him? That shut her up a while." (5.48)

Miss Maudie's joke embarrasses Miss Stephanie into holding her tongue, but perhaps it's effective because it plays off the truth of Miss Stephanie's desire to know everyone's intimate secrets as well as if she were sleeping with them.

Jem and Scout count Miss Maudie as a friend because, unlike most adults, she treats them with respect. If the best she can say of Atticus is that he is "the same in his house as he is on the public streets" (5.54), Miss Maudie has the rare ability to act the same to children as she does to adults: "She had never told on us, had never played cat-and-mouse with us, she was not at all interested in our private lives" (5.36). While Miss Stephanie is always poking and prying, especially at Scout, and Mrs. Merriweather can't even speak to children in the same tone of voice she uses for grown-ups, Miss Maudie sees the kids as slightly-less-experienced adults, and treats them like that.

And Miss Maudie's equal-opportunity respect extends to African-Americans, too. When Aunt Alexandra is depressed and bitter over the townspeople's leaving Atticus to do the right thing all by his lonesome, Miss Maudie speaks up for the small group of like-minded people in Maycomb.

"The handful of people in this town who say that fair play is not marked White Only; the handful of people who say a fair trial is for everybody, not just us; the handful of people with enough humility to think, when they look at a Negro, there but for the Lord's kindness am I." (24.81)

Like Atticus's constant advice to Scout to put herself in the other person's shoes, Miss Maudie's respect for others is based on sympathy. Unlike Atticus, she can't be a lawyer or face down a lynch mob (or maybe she could), but perhaps her local influence is still potent despite being exercised in tea parties rather than courtrooms, and provides an example to Scout of how being a lady doesn't necessarily mean having your selfhood squished out of you.

Heck Tate Character Analysis

As sheriff of Maycomb County, Heck Tate's official role is maintaining law and order. Through most of the book, however, he seems about as powerful as Ranger Smith faced with Yogi Bear and a missing picnic basket. When the mad dog turns up on Scout's street, Tate hands the gun to Atticus rather than risking sending a stray bullet into the Radley house with his own shot (see "Mad Dog" in "Symbols, Imagery, Allegory" for more on this scene). When Ewell accuses Tom Robinson of raping Mayella, Tate has to arrest him despite the lack of evidence. And when Tom is held in the Maycomb jail the night before the trial, Tate not only warns Atticus in advance that even as sheriff he might not be able to protect Tom, he also gets tricked into going off on a wild goose chase, leaving Atticus to face down the lynch mob without official backup.

After all these counts of impotence, at the end of the novel Tate faces off against Atticus, and wins, in the matter of Ewell's death.

"I never heard tell that it's against the law for a citizen to do his utmost to prevent a crime from being committed, which is exactly what he did, but maybe you'll say it's my duty to tell the town all about it and not hush it up. Know what'd happen then? All the ladies in Maycomb includin' my wife'd be knocking on his door bringing angel food cakes. To my way of thinkin', Mr. Finch, taking the one man who's done you and this town a great service an' draggin' him with his shy ways into the limelight – to me, that's a sin. It's a sin and I'm not about to have it on my head. If it was any other man, it'd be different. But not this man, Mr. Finch. […]

"I may not be much, Mr. Finch, but I'm still sheriff of Maycomb County and Bob Ewell fell on his knife. Good night, sir." (30.62-63)

While on the one hand, Tate's decision goes against the letter of the law, on the other, it follows a different law, which Tate believes to be the higher one. Depending on whether or not we agree with his decision, Tate is either doing the right thing or weakening the rule of law (or both) – he acts on moral grounds, but in doing so he goes against Atticus's ideal of equality under the law. Perhaps one message of Heck Tate's character, and Link Deas's as well, is that until that ideal becomes more of a reality, people should do what they can to bring fairness at least a little bit closer, even when the law's not on their side. That same principle, however, justifies the lynch mob's attempt to enact vigilante justice on Tom.

Link Deas Character Analysis

While Mr. Deas at first seems on the side of order over truth (his telling Atticus that he has "everything to lose" from defending Tom brings out Atticus's notoriously dangerous response, "Do you really think so?" [15.20-21]), later he becomes one of the few people who are willing to take action on Tom's behalf, speaking out in his favor at the trial.

Mr. Link Deas rose from the audience and announced: 'I just want the whole lot of you to know one thing right now. That boy's worked for me eight years an' I ain't had a speck o'trouble outa him. Not a speck."

"Shut your mouth, sir!" *Judge Taylor was wide awake and roaring. [...] "Link Deas," he yelled, "if you have anything you want to say you can say it under oath and at the proper time, but until then you get out of this room, you hear me? [...] I'll be damned if I'll listen to this case again!" (19.89-90)*

While on the one hand it's admirable that Mr. Deas wants to support Tom, in speaking out of turn he risks causing a mistrial, which could put Tom in more danger by drawing out the process even further. But since even with a trial that follows the rules of order, Tom is unjustly convicted, perhaps Mr. Deas has the right idea in breaking the rules to speak on the side of truth.

After Tom is killed, Mr. Deas continues his support of Tom's family. He creates a job for Helen even though he doesn't really need her help, as a personal attempt to make up for the injustice of the system. While he doesn't do much to change the ways in which the system is broken, he does make a significant difference in the life of Helen and her children by protecting her from Ewell.

"As Mr. Link came out of his store he saw Mr. Ewell leaning on the fence. Mr. Ewell said, "Don't you look at me, Link Deas, like I was dirt. I ain't jumped your-"

"First thing you can do, Ewell, is get your stinkin' carcass off my property. You're leanin' on it an' I can't afford fresh paint for it. Second thing you can do is stay away from my cook or I'll

have you up for assault-"

"I ain't touched her, Link Deas, and ain't about to go with no nigger!"

"You don't have to touch her, all you have to do is make her afraid, an' if assault ain't enough to keep you locked up awhile, I'll get you in on the Ladies' Law, so get outa my sight! If you don't think I mean it, just bother that girl again!"

Mr. Ewell evidently thought he meant it, for Helen reported no further trouble. (27.8-12)

Ewell tries to hide behind the letter of the law by not staying away from actions that are obviously criminal, but Mr. Deas sees what he's really trying to do: terrorize Helen in a way that might make her stay home or leave Maycomb altogether. Mr. Deas's threats raise the question of what would have happened if Helen herself had taken the matter up with the law (though after what happened to her husband, it's not surprising she doesn't want to): would she have been able to get effective support without a white man backing her? Like Tom, it seems that for Helen her legal rights are dependent not on what the law says but on the white men who enforce the laws, or fail to do so. While Mr. Deas does act on the side of justice, making Helen's safety dependent on him raises the question of what would have happened if he hadn't been willing to take on Ewell.

Mrs. Henry Lafayette Dubose Character Analysis

Boo may be the ghost of Scout's neighborhood, but Mrs. Dubose is the dragon. Scout introduces her as "plain hell" (1.14)

Jem and I hated her. If she was on the porch when we passed, we would be raked by her wrathful gaze, subjected to ruthless interrogation regarding our behavior, and given a melancholy prediction on what we would amount to when we grew up, which was always nothing. (11.3)

Despite being confined to a wheelchair most of the time, Mrs. Dubose has the power to inspire rage and fear just through the power of her words. Closer up, her appearance alone is enough to gross Scout out.

Cords of saliva would collect on her lips; she would draw them in, then open her mouth again. Her mouth seemed to have a private existence of its own. It worked separate and apart from the rest of her, out and in, like a clam hole at low tide. Occasionally it would say, "Pt," like some viscous substance coming to a boil. (11.86)

For Scout, Mrs. Dubose is a distressing object, a force that takes over their afternoons after Jem goes crazy on her camellias, barely human. It's not until after she dies that Scout and Jem get a sense of what's going on behind the drool and venom: Mrs. Dubose is a morphine addict who had vowed to go clean before she died, and enlisted Jem and Scout (without their knowledge) to keep her off the stuff for longer and longer periods of time. Atticus tells the kids the lesson he hopes they've learned from her.

"I wanted you to see what real courage is, instead of getting the idea that courage is a man with a gun in his hand. It's when you know you're licked before you begin but you begin anyway and you see it through no matter what. You rarely win, but sometimes you do. Mrs. Dubose won, all ninety-eight pounds of her. According to her views, she died beholden to nothing and nobody. She was the bravest person I ever knew." (11.*)

Even though no one would have blamed Mrs. Dubose if she had wanted to leave this world in narcotic bliss, she decided to try to do what she felt was right, no matter how impossible it seemed or how painful it was. Hmm, sounds like a person whose name begins with "A" and ends with "tticus." Overcoming Mrs. Dubose is a valuable experience for both Jem and Scout as they move unknowingly towards the Robinson trial, though it's unclear whether admiring her bravery or learning to brave her cantankerousness without exploding is the more useful lesson.

Caroline Fisher Character Analysis

As an outsider to Maycomb (she comes from the strange and far-off land of northern Alabama), Miss Caroline gets as many lessons from her students as she gives to them. As a main booster for the school's new educational system (what Jem calls the "Dewey Decimal System" [2.25]), she's a representative of the confusing world outside, and reinforces the idea that Maycomb is its own little world. She is utterly unable to cope when Scout's reading and writing exceed first grade standards: "We don't write in the first grade, we print. You won't learn to write until you're in the third grade" (2.26). The absurdity of her must-follow-the-rules attitude suggests that a smarter approach is to adapt the rules when necessary; on the other hand, in facing off with her Scout learns that sometimes when stupid rules won't bend you just have to make a show of following them to get by.

John Hale Finch Character Analysis

Uncle Jack is the uncle of Jem and Scout, who always look forward to his visits. He's a joker who is friendly with the kids, but, being unmarried with no children of his own, doesn't really know how to treat them fairly. Scout points this out when he punishes her for beating up Francis without letting her tell her side of the story; when he hears what she has to say, he's ready to go beat up Francis himself, and possibly Aunt Alexandra to boot. Uncle Jack's willingness to admit he was wrong, and his loyalty in keeping his word to Scout (he promises not to tell Atticus why she was fighting Francis), put him in the category of adults who treat children with respect (along with Atticus and Miss Maudie). His interactions with Scout suggest some ways in which the differences between adults and children can be bridged to the benefit of both.

Grace Merriweather Character Analysis

A heavily religious woman and a closet drinker, Mrs. Grace Merriweather is "the most devout lady in Maycomb" (24.25). Her devoutness shows itself in her commitment to saving the Mrunas, an implied-to-be-African tribe, or at least to talking up their white savior, J. Grimes Everett. She's also committed to making sure her African-American servants live Christian lives.

"Gertrude, I tell you there's nothing more distracting than a sulky darky. Their mouths go down to here. Just ruins your day to have one of 'em in the kitchen. You know what I said to my Sophy, Gertrude? I said, 'Sophy,' I said, 'you simply are not being a Christian today. Jesus Christ never went around grumbling and complaining,' and you know, it did her good. She took her eyes off that floor and said, 'Nome, Miz Merriweather, Jesus never went around grumblin'.' I tell you, Gertrude, you never ought to let an opportunity go by to witness for the Lord." (24.43)

The fact that Jesus also never went around telling people to stop acting so cranky because it gets on His nerves seems to have escaped Mrs. Merriweather, as does the idea that kindness begins at home – if she devoted all the energy she currently spends on J. Grimes Everett and his far-off Mrunas on being considerate of the less-fortunate closer to home, Maycomb might be a better place.

Mrs. Merriweather also conceives, writes, directs, produces, narrates, and stars in the school's Halloween pageant, and doesn't forget to tell Scout afterwards that she ruined it all by making her entrance late, suggesting that her lack of sympathy isn't limited to her African-American servants.

Reverend Sykes Character Analysis

As minister of First Purchase Church, Reverend Sykes is an authority figure in Maycomb's African-American community. Like Santa Claus, he's knows if you been bad or good: at the service Scout and Jem attend, he's not afraid to name names when it comes to the sinners in his congregation. And he's not above coercing the congregation into being good for goodness' sake, holding them hostage in the hot church until they cough up the ten dollars Helen Robinson needs to feed her family for the week. The way he does things seems weird to Scout and Jem, but its effectiveness shows them that the white people's ways they're familiar with aren't necessarily the only ones that work.

When Scout, Jem, and Dill watch the Robinson trial from the "colored" balcony, Reverend Sykes is the only African-American person who speaks to them or who is even named. Even when the entire balcony stands to honor Atticus after the trial, Reverend Sykes serves as the voice of the silent group, explaining what's going on not only to Scout but also to the reader. What effect does making a major mouthpiece of the African-Americans in the novel a considerate preacher have on how the reader perceives that community? Why do the other African-Americans, besides Calpurnia, lack much of a voice in the novel?

While the character of Reverend Sykes suggests that the African-American community has its own organization invisible to the white residents, Scout's position as first-person narrator means that we as readers can only access that organization filtered through a white person's perspective. The novel from the point of view of Reverend Sykes would be very different indeed.

Judge John Taylor Character Analysis

Scout calls Judge Taylor "a sleepy old shark" (16.105), and the description suits him well: he may seem out of it most of the time, but disrupt his court in any way and he's on it like a shark on fishmeat.

While he seems fairly even-handed in court, his personal views on the Robinson case come out in more subtle ways. He's the one who appoints Atticus as Tom's defense council even when the job should have gone to another, less experienced, man. Later, Atticus says that the judge looked at Ewell on the witness stand "as if he were a three-legged chicken or a square egg" and continues, "Don't tell me judges don't try to prejudice juries" (27.16). Despite these attempts to influence the outcome of the case, Judge Taylor is ultimately powerless to prevent the jury from finding Tom guilty on circumstantial evidence. Like Atticus, he works within the system, but it seems that ultimately he can't overcome the ways in which the system itself is broken.

Dolphus Raymond Character Analysis

Mr. Raymond is a borderline figure who confuses Maycomb's neat social and racial categories. In the strictly segregated crowds outside the courthouse, he sits with the African-Americans, and Jem tells Scout and Dill that he's had several children with an African-American woman – despite being from an old, rich family. Or perhaps it's being from an old, rich family that allows him to live how he likes without worrying about what other people think.

Later, Scout and Dill find out that Mr. Raymond does care about what other people think, but not in the way they expected. His paper bag turns out to be hiding not whisky but Coke, and his constant drunkenness is a put-on. He explains to the kids why he does it: "When I come to town, [...] if I weave a little and drink out of this sack, folks can say Dolphus Raymond's in the clutches of whiskey – that's why he won't change his ways. He can't help himself, that's why he lives the way he does" (20.15). Like Calpurnia's speaking one language at home with the Finches and another at the African-American Church, Mr. Raymond's double life shows Scout the compromises people have to make in order to live in communities where they don't quite fit in.

Braxton Bragg Underwood Character Analysis

Mr. Underwood shares his name with a famous typewriter brand – appropriate, since he runs Maycomb's one and only newspaper, *The Maycomb Tribune*. He's also one of the few minor characters in the novel who changes over the course of the story. After one of his first appearances, covering Atticus with a shotgun the night the lynch mob tries to take Tom out of jail, Atticus explains why this was a weird thing for Mr. Bragg to do: "he despises Negroes, won't have one near him" (16.5), and yet he acts to protect Tom as well as Atticus. After Tom is killed, Mr. Bragg writes a bitter editorial about the injustice of his fate, suggesting that his attitudes towards African-Americans have changed – or perhaps that racist attitudes can be more complicated than a simple for or against.

Walter Cunningham Sr. Character Analysis

Mr. Cunningham is the father of Walter Cunningham, Scout's classmate. He's also a client of Atticus's, and pays Atticus for his services in goods rather than money, because that's all he can afford. In the eyes of Maycomb, the Cunninghams are a step below the townspeople (they're poor farmers), but a step above the Ewells (they proudly eke out enough to survive from the land rather than going on welfare).

Mr. Cunningham, along with others like him, is part of the mob that tries to lynch Tom Robinson the night before the trial, putting him on the side of regressive and prejudiced values. When Scout talks to him about his son, however, he turns back and takes the rest of the mob with him. At the trial, Mr. Cunningham's double first cousin is the only one willing to acquit Tom. Mr. Cunningham and his family suggest that at least some kinds of discrimination and violence come out of ignorance, and that experience can open eyes and change minds – at least sometimes.

Walter Cunningham Jr. Character Analysis

Walter is almost as old as Jem but is in Scout's class at school. On the first day of first grade he lacks both shoes and a lunch, but it's clear he's a step up from Burris Ewell, since Walter at least has clean clothes. Scout tries to explain Walter's lack of a lunch and refusal of a loan to the teacher since Walter himself can't or won't, but Walter's situation (too poor to pay back a quarter) is simply beyond Miss Caroline's ability to understand. Scout's own ability to understand is exceeded when Walter pours molasses all over his lunch at the Finches, and she learns from Cal that just because someone's different doesn't mean she gets to judge them. Scout gets a lesson in the other direction when she wants to hang out with Walter but Aunt Alexandra squashes that idea because the Cunninghams, in her eyes, are trash. Walter, as a Cunningham at Scout's age level, serves as her gateway into the complex world of white class relations in Maycomb.

Helen Robinson Character Analysis

As Tom's wife, Helen suffers from the persecution of her husband. After his arrest, she has difficulty finding work, and it's only the concern of Reverend Sykes and the kindness of Link Deas that enable her to support her family. When she hears of Tom's death, she is devastated: Dill says she "just fell down in the dirt, like a giant with a big foot just came along and stepped on her" (25.23). When Ewell harasses her on her way to work for Mr. Deas, she doesn't want her boss to get involved, suggesting that after her experiences with Tom's trial she just wants to attract as little attention as possible, but he does anyway. Helen's main function in the novel is in relation to Tom: other than making Tom's character more believable and sympathetic, and showing the wide-ranging impact of the Ewells' accusation, she doesn't have much to do.

Miss Stephanie Crawford Character Analysis

As the town busybody, Miss Stephanie makes it her business to spread gossip, the meaner the better. She's the Finch kids' main source of rumors about Boo Radley, and takes as much delight in the ghoulish details as Jem does. Occasionally she tries to hide her unladylike curiosity, like when she pretends that she's going into town for any other reason than to watch the Robinson trial, but most of the time she doesn't do much to disguise the fact that she knows more up-to-the-minute dirt than Facebook. Miss Stephanie doesn't change much if at all over the course of the novel, but attitudes towards her do change: Scout in particular learns to withstand her snarky comments without letting them get to her, showing that she's a little bit closer to growing up into a lady.

Horace Gilmer Character Analysis

Assigned the prosecution of the Tom Robinson case, Mr. Gilmer faces off against Atticus in court. While Scout thinks their rivalry is strictly a legal one, Dill is disturbed by the difference in the two men's approach to the trial: while Atticus treats all the witnesses, even the Ewells, with respect, Mr. Gilmer treats Tom Robinson with a rudeness and contempt he doesn't show to the white witnesses. We only see Mr. Gilmer in court, so it's hard to say if he really sees Tom that way or if he's just putting on a show to win his case.

Lula Character Analysis

Lula appears only once in the novel, but even though brief her presence is memorable. When Calpurnia takes Jem and Scout to the African-American First Purchase Church, Lula is the one person who doesn't roll out the welcome mat for the Finch kids. In fact, Lula is the lone African-American voice of anything approaching dangerous anger in the novel.

Her opposition to the presence of Jem and Scout at First Purchase has some validity, even though it's immediately silenced – after all, they're white people invading a sanctuary that has been painfully carved out of a white realm in which African-Americans are second-class citizens. The momentary flare-up of Lula suggests an alternate response, rage, that the African-Americans of Maycomb could be having to the events in their town, and raises the question of why she's the only one who doesn't appear quietly resigned. Are the others concerned about the very real dangers that any behavior seen as threatening would bring down on their heads, or is the novel itself unable to allow such disturbing emotions into its carefully-controlled portrayal of African-American harmlessness? It's hard to say from Lula's brief appearance, but she does make the novel's portrayal of African-Americans more complicated.

Nathan Radley Character Analysis

Boo's brother, Mr. Nathan takes the place of their father when he dies. Whether he's Boo's jailor or protector is unclear. Equally unclear is his reason for filling up the knothole where Boo leaves gifts for the kids – does he want to keep his brother from making connections with the outside world, or just prevent him from getting hurt by thoughtless children? He does seem to see his yard as his own live-action version of Grand Theft Auto – when Jem, Dill, and Scout sneak up to the house at midnight trying to catch a glimpse of Boo, Mr. Nathan meets them with a shotgun blast. On the other hand, he helps save some of Miss Maudie's possessions when her house catches on fire. Though we see more of him than Boo, Mr. Nathan is just as much of a mystery – no one really knows what makes him tick.

Character Roles

Protagonist
Scout Finch
Scout tells the story, but that by itself isn't enough to make her the protagonist. She also *is* the story: while many of the novel's major events happen around her rather than to her, it's her coming-of-age that brings these events together into a narrative. Other characters also develop and change over the course of the story – Jem, Atticus, even Aunt Alexandra – but the novel keeps coming back to Scout, and how these changes affect her own path towards adulthood.

Antagonist
Bob Ewell
Ewell is nasty. He doesn't have one redeeming characteristic. While Mayella is the one whose actions first get Tom into trouble, Ewell is the one who makes sure that that trouble snowballs into a court case, conviction, and execution. Even after the case is over, Ewell keeps going after Atticus, Judge Taylor, and Helen Robinson, and finally almost kills the Finch kids. Heck Tate probably wasn't exaggerating when he said the ladies of Maycomb would bury Boo in cake for taking Ewell out: this guy is bad news without a glimmer of good.

Guide/Mentor
Atticus Finch

As their father, Atticus is supposed to provide guidance to Jem and Scout, but he does an exceptionally good job of it. He isn't afraid to speak honestly to his kids, and even explains what rape is to Scout when she asks. Atticus not only talks to his children about what he wants to teach them and why, he also tries to provide a good example to them in his own conduct. In practicing what he preaches, Atticus shows his kids that such behavior is not only desirable, but possible. And as the ethical center of the book, Atticus gives the reader a moral compass with which to navigate the shifting sands of Maycomb values.

Foil

Tom Robinson/Boo Radley

At first glance, Tom and Boo seem very different: one lives with his wife and children among friends, the other lives in isolation with his taciturn brother. One has his fellow churchgoers take up a collection on his behalf, while the other has no one think much about him except some curious kids. But dig deeper, and Tom and Boo start to look more similar: both are disabled in some way (Tom's crippled arm, Boo's crippling shyness), both are innocents with a bad reputation, and both are compared to mockingbirds. Perhaps most tellingly, Tom and Boo both serve as scapegoats for their community, being blamed for things they didn't do. As foils, they reveal less about each other than about the community they live in, and suggest that the people a community includes say less about it than those whom it excludes.

Character Clues

Actions

While characters may say all kinds of things, it's what they do that shows what they're really made of. Example: Atticus says that Mr. Underwood "despises Negroes, won't have one near him" (16.5), but when a lynch mob threatens both Tom and Atticus, Mr. Underwood is waiting with his shotgun to defend them. And after Tom's death, Mr. Underwood's editorial in *The Maycomb Tribune* takes a much stronger stance in Tom's favor than most Maycomb citizens are willing to hold to.

Direct Characterization

The novel often sums up its characters in a few words: Miss Stephanie Crawford is "a neighborhood scold" (1.50), Boo Radley is "a malevolent phantom" (1.43), and Mrs. Dubose is "plain hell" (1.14). While these capsule descriptions are sometimes accurate, most of them become more complex and nuanced through the other "Tools of Characterization" as the book progresses, suggesting that people are rarely as simple as they might seem at first.

Family Life

Aunt Alexandra believes each family has a "streak" (13.26), but characters' home lives do just as much to show what they're like. When Scout says to Miss Maudie, "Atticus don't ever do anything to Jem and me in the house that he don't do in the yard" (5.53), it tells us that Atticus cares more about actually doing right than just making people believe that he does so. The image that Atticus builds up at Tom's trial of Mayella's depressing home life tells the reader as well as the jury that she's terribly lonely, and might latch on to anyone who shows her a moment's kindness. And part of the mystery of Boo is wondering about how he lives at home:

whether his house is a sanctuary or a prison, and whether his family is his protectors or his jailors.

Location

The first warning bell that signals to Scout that she and Miss Caroline might have some difficulty communicating is that the teacher is from North Alabama, on the other side of the state from Maycomb. Even within Maycomb, where a character lives tells you something about them (for a different take on Maycomb's geography, see "Setting"). The Ewells don't live by the dump just because it's cheap, but because they're Trash. The Cunninghams out in the woods are on the fringes of Maycomb society as well as geography, and live a self-sufficient existence that doesn't have much to do with the town itself. (And the Cunningham's settlement, Old Sarum, shares its name with an early English village, suggesting that they look more to the past than the future.)

Speech and Dialogue

How a character talks can often tell you more than what they say. In racially-divided Maycomb, one word in particular is a marker of where a character stands: "nigger."

The word first appears in the text when Scout echoes something Calpurnia said, showing from the start that its usage is more complicated that just a nasty way for whites to put down African-Americans: Calpurnia isn't looking forward to hip-hop and reclaiming the word, but using it to talk about a particular kind of African-American person. Calpurnia uses the term again when she's addressing Lula, showing it has power as an insult even within Maycomb's African-American community. Calpurnia's use of the word suggests her sense of difference from that community (what Scout calls her "double life" [12.138]), but also raises questions about attitudes towards race among African-Americans in Maycomb that the novel doesn't really address.

Atticus never uses the word "nigger," except when he's explaining to Scout why she shouldn't say it, or why she shouldn't get into fights when other people call Atticus a "nigger-lover."

"Scout," said Atticus, "nigger-lover is just one of those terms that don't mean anything – like snot-nose. It's hard to explain – ignorant, trashy people use it when they think somebody's favoring Negroes over and above themselves. It's slipped into usage with some people like ourselves, when they want a common, ugly term to label somebody." (11.107)

Is Atticus right? Does the term really have no meaning except as a way to put others down? Whether the answer to these questions is yes or no, the common usage of "nigger" in the text speaks not only to the attributes of individual characters, but also of the norms of the community in which they live.

Literary Devices

Symbols, Imagery, Allegory

Mockingbirds

The title of the book is *To Kill a Mockingbird*, so mockingbirds must be important, right? But why? Let's look at a few passages to try to figure out some answers to that question.

Mockingbirds first appear when Jem and Scout are learning how to use their shiny new air rifles. Atticus won't teach them how to shoot, but he does give them one rule to follow.

Atticus said to Jem one day, "I'd rather you shot at tin cans in the back yard, but I know you'll go after birds. Shoot all the bluejays you want, if you can hit 'em, but remember it's a sin to kill a mockingbird."

That was the only time I ever heard Atticus say it was a sin to do something, and I asked Miss Maudie about it.

"Your father's right," she said. "Mockingbirds don't do one thing but make music for us to enjoy. They don't eat up people's gardens, don't nest in corncribs, they don't do one thing but sing their hearts out for us. That's why it's a sin to kill a mockingbird." (10.7)

So, mockingbirds are harmless, innocent creatures, and killing them is wrong, because they don't hurt anyone. (The same could be said for cows, but hamburgers are so tasty, while mockingbirds presumably aren't.) But is this lesson so important in itself that it's worth putting it front and center on the cover of the book? There must be more going on here.

Mr. Underwood's editorial after the death of Tom Robinson doesn't mention mockingbirds by name, but it does have a similar message.

Mr. Underwood didn't talk about miscarriages of justice, he was writing so children could understand. Mr. Underwood simply figured it was a sin to kill cripples, be they standing, sitting, or escaping. He likened Tom's death to the senseless slaughter of songbirds by hunters and children, and Maycomb thought he was trying to write an editorial poetical enough to be reprinted in The Montgomery Advertiser. *(25.27)*

Mr. Underwood may be trying to get through to even the stupidest residents of Maycomb, but his editorial also makes sure that every reader gets the connection: the mockingbird and Tom are in the same class of beings. But what's the reason for bringing the bird and the man together? Mr. Underwood says it's because of Tom's disability, though it's unclear why he thinks that makes a difference (perhaps it's along the lines of "women and children first": those thought to be weak should receive special protection). Perhaps Tom's innocence of the crime he's accused of makes him similar to the mockingbird who does no harm to anyone. Or perhaps it's the senselessness that's really key: killing Tom brought about no good and prevented no evil, just like shooting a mockingbird.

The idea of killing a mockingbird turns up once more in the book, when Scout is telling Atticus she understands about not dragging Boo into court.

Atticus looked like he needed cheering up. I ran to him and hugged him and kissed him with all my might. "Yes sir, I understand," I reassured him. "Mr. Tate was right."

Atticus disengaged himself and looked at me. "What do you mean?"

"Well, it'd be sort of like shootin' a mockingbird, wouldn't it?" (30.66-68)

Stories of poisoned pecans aside, all Boo does is watch the neighborhood, leave trinkets for Jem and Scout, and act to protect them when they're attacked. Like killing a mockingbird, arresting Boo would serve no useful purpose, and harm someone who never meant anyone any harm. So over the course of the novel, killing mockingbirds is associated with the sinful, the pointless, and the cruel.

What's the effect of using the mockingbird in this way? On the one hand, linking particular characters to mockingbirds reduces them to the level of animals; on the other, it says that even animals are worthy of sympathy and the respect of being left alone if they're doing the same to you. By making killing mockingbirds a clear-cut case of wanton destruction, the book creates a rule for judging more complicated situations: bringing in the mockingbird is a prompt to take a step back from knee-jerk reactions (escaped convicts must be shot! murderers must be arrested!) and ask, what benefit is there? Why do this? What does it accomplish?

No mockingbirds were harmed in the making of this module.

The Radley Place

If Maycomb were Disneyland, the Radley Place would be the Haunted Mansion. And the Finch kids aren't the only ones who avoid it like the plague.

A Negro would not pass the Radley Place at night, he would cut across to the sidewalk opposite and whistle as he walked. The Maycomb school grounds adjoined the back of the Radley lot; from the Radley chickenyard tall pecan trees shook their fruit into the schoolyard, but the nuts lay untouched by the children: Radley pecans would kill you. A baseball hit into the Radley yard was a lost ball and no questions asked. (1.43)

What makes the Radley Place so frightening? Part of it is, of course, its most famous occupant, Boo Radley.

Inside the house lived a malevolent phantom. People said he existed, but Jem and I had never seen him. People said he went out at night when the moon was down, and peeped in windows. When people's azaleas froze in a cold snap, it was because he had breathed on them. Any stealthy small crimes committed in Maycomb were his work. (1.43)

Boo becomes a figure of superstition, a convenient excuse for bad things happening. Perhaps the house takes on such an evil reputation because Boo is never seen; when the kids look for him, all they ever see is the outside of the house, which becomes almost a stand-in for Boo himself. And like Boo, the house is isolated from the community it sits in the middle of.

The shutters and doors of the Radley house were closed on Sundays, another thing alien to Maycomb's ways: closed doors meant illness and cold weather only. Of all days Sunday was the day for formal afternoon visiting: ladies wore corsets, men wore coats, children wore shoes. But to climb the Radley front steps and call, "He-y," of a Sunday afternoon was something their neighbors never did. The Radley house had no screen doors. I once asked Atticus if it ever had any; Atticus said yes, but before I was born. (1.45)

The reclusiveness of all the residents of the Radley House, not just Boo, means that it's a kind of black hole in the neighborhood, a house of mystery in the midst of the familiar. Perhaps the Finch kids and Dill spend so much time trying to make sense of the Radley Place, and the Radleys, because they don't understand why anyone would voluntarily isolate themselves. If Maycomb is such a great place to live, why do the Radleys purposely keep themselves out of it? Is there something wrong with the Radleys, or something wrong with the community that they can't or won't be a part of? Why do they act so differently from everyone else?

When Scout finally gets to the threshold of the Radley Place after Boo rescues her and her brother from Ewell, she does an odd thing. Instead of peering through the window to try to see inside the house that's intrigued the kids for so long, she turns around and looks outward.

In daylight, I thought, you could see to the postoffice corner.

Daylight... in my mind, the night faded.[...] It was summertime, and two children scampered down the sidewalk toward a man approaching in the distance. The man waved, and the children raced each other to him.

It was still summertime, and the children came closer. A boy trudged down the sidewalk dragging a fishingpole behind him. A man stood waiting with his hands on his hips. Summertime, and his children played in the front yard with their friend, enacting a strange little drama of their own invention.

It was fall, and his children fought on the sidewalk in front of Mrs. Dubose's. The boy helped his sister to her feet, and they made their way home. Fall, and his children trotted to and fro around the corner, the day's woes and triumphs on their faces. They stopped at an oak tree, delighted, puzzled, apprehensive.

Winter, and his children shivered at the front gate, silhouetted against a blazing house. Winter, and a man walked into the street, dropped his glasses, and shot a dog.

Summer, and he watched his children's heart break. Autumn again, and Boo's children needed him.

Atticus was right. One time he said you never really know a man until you stand in his shoes and walk around in them. Just standing on the Radley porch was enough. (31.25-31)

Scout realizes the Radley Place is like one-way glass: even though the kids couldn't see in, Boo could see out, and perhaps was just as interested in them as they were in him. Does this make Boo a part of the community after all? On the one hand, he watched what everyone else was doing like a spectator at a play. On the other, he was able to break the fourth wall and step in when he was needed. At the end of the novel, Boo disappears once more into the Radley Place, and Scout says that they never saw him again. But perhaps with her knowledge of what the world looks like from inside it, Scout will now see the Radley Place as a living house instead of a dead one.

The Mad Dog

Meet Tim Johnson. He was just snuffling along, investigating interesting smells, burying bones only to dig them up again, and looking out for lady dogs, when – bam – the symbolic structure of the book picks him up and decrees he has to die. Why? What did poor Tim the Dog ever do to get infected with rabies and be gunned down like, well, a dog?

For starters, there's his name. It may seem odd to give an animal the last name of the family it belongs to, but it's apparently common practice in Maycomb – Judge Taylor's pooch gets the same treatment. But more interestingly, it allows the dog's name to sound suspiciously like that of another character. Tim Johnson…Tom Robinson? Coincidence? Perhaps. But Scout's memory of her father shooting the dog does pop up more than once in situations involving Tom, and doesn't get mentioned otherwise.

For example, after Scout turns away the lynch mob, her memory of Atticus in front of the jail merges with her memory of him shooting the dog.

I was very tired, and was drifting into sleep when the memory of Atticus calmly folding his newspaper and pushing back his hat became Atticus standing in the middle of an empty waiting street, pushing up his glasses. The full meaning of the night's events hit me and I began crying. (16.3)

But why does Scout associate the two images? Perhaps they're both examples of Atticus doing tough things he doesn't want to do. Or of Atticus facing off with a mindless threat. (He does later refer to the men in the lynch mob as "animals" [16.22]).

Scout returns to this memory again when she's dozing off, waiting for the jury to announce its verdict in Tom's case.

The feeling grew until the atmosphere in the courtroom was exactly the same as a cold February morning, when the mockingbirds were still, and the carpenters had stopped hammering on Miss Maudie's new house, and every wood door in the neighborhood was shut as tight as the doors of the Radley Place. A deserted, waiting, empty street, and the courtroom was packed with people. A steaming summer night was no different from a winter morning. […]. I expected Mr. Tate to say any minute, "Take him, Mr. Finch...." (21.46)

Why does Scout have this feeling? In both past and present, she's waiting for something to happen; both times, she has no power over the outcome. In the previous instance, Atticus's skill with a gun was able to save the neighborhood from the mad dog; will he be able to do the same this time? The same image recurs once more as the jury delivers their verdict.

I saw something only a lawyer's child could be expected to see, could be expected to watch for, and it was like watching Atticus walk into the street, raise a rifle to his shoulder and pull the trigger, but watching all the time knowing that the gun was empty. A jury never looks at a defendant it has convicted, and when this jury came in, not one of them looked at Tom Robinson. (21.48)

Even Atticus's talent for sharp-shooting can't do anything if the gun isn't loaded. It's tempting to try to map out the symbolism here – is the gun the legal process? are the bullets the jury? is Tim Johnson racism? – but that might be an oversimplification. Perhaps it's just the feeling Scout has that's the link between the two situations – the sick horror at what's happening, but knowing that it can't be any other way.

Setting

Maycomb, Alabama in the 1930s

To Kill a Mockingbird takes place in the fictional small Southern town of Maycomb in the 1930s (Tom's trial takes place in 1935). Slavery and the Civil War of the 1860s still loom large in the rearview mirror, but the civil rights movement of the 1950s and 60s is just a speck on the future horizon.

Maycomb, despite its civic importance as the county seat, is a small and stagnant town. It's a place where time seems to stand still.

A day was twenty-four hours long but seemed longer. There was no hurry, for there was nowhere to go, nothing to buy and no money to buy it with, nothing to see outside the boundaries of Maycomb County. (1.10)

Maycomb is its own little world that doesn't know what's happening elsewhere and doesn't care. Few people move there (not much reason to) and few people leave (why bother). This stagnation means that the same families have been around for generations, and family reputations have entered into the local lore as immovable facts.

Thus the dicta No Crawford Minds His Own Business, Every Third Merriweather Is Morbid, The Truth Is Not in the Delafields, All the Bufords Walk Like That, were simply guides to daily living: never take a check from a Delafield without a discreet call to the bank; Miss Maudie Atkinson's shoulder stoops because she was a Buford; if Mrs. Grace Merriweather sips gin out of Lydia E. Pinkham bottles it's nothing unusual – her mother did the same. (13.32)

It's unclear whether these stereotypes are accurate descriptions of family traits, passed down through inheritance or parenting, or self-fulfilling prophecies – either because people act the way others expect them to, or others see what they expect to see. But the differences between the various town families, whether real or imagined, pale when the town is set against the groups haunting its margins. Jem comes up with his own classification of the various species of *Homo Maycombis*:

"There's four kinds of folks in the world. There's the ordinary kind like us and the neighbors, there's the kind like the Cunninghams out in the woods, the kind like the Ewells down at the dump, and the Negroes." (23.103)

Neither system leaves much room for individuality and independent thought, let alone breaking with the past and striking off in a new direction. The way things are in Maycomb is the way things have always been, and there's not much anyone can do about it.

And the way things have always been is racially segregated. Racism, as Atticus says after he loses the Robinson case, is "just as much Maycomb County as missionary teas" (22.11), and it's displayed even in the geography of the town. The African-Americans have their own settlement on the outskirts of white Maycomb, and their own church and cemetery outside the city limits. At Tom's trial the African-Americans sit on one side of the town square, and the whites on the other. Inside the courtroom, the whites have the good seats on the floor while the African-Americans are up in the balcony. It's like the town is one big middle school dance, except that one side has all the power of teachers and then some, and the other has even more limitations than students. Other than a few border-crosses like Mr. Dolph Raymond, whites and blacks in Maycomb don't live together, pray together, eat together, or even die together.

So in this town where separate is definitely not equal, for Atticus to act as if Tom Robinson as just as much right to a fair trial as if his skin were white makes some people angrily upset at having to share their rights with people they think don't deserve it, as if human rights were a cake with a limited number of slices. Others are more disturbed that Bob Ewell is able to make the court enforce his false accusation. While the anti-Tom Maycomb is the dominant one, the tiny pro-Tom faction refuses to be erased from the town community.

"The handful of people in this town who say that fair play is not marked White Only; the handful of people who say a fair trial is for everybody, not just us; the handful of people with enough humility to think, when they look at a Negro, there but for the Lord's kindness am I." Miss Maudie's old crispness was returning: "The handful of people in this town with background, that's who they are." (24.81)

This "handful of people" can't save Tom Robinson, but perhaps they can put Maycomb a little farther forward on the road to the civil rights era.

Narrator Point of View

First Person (Central Narrator)

Our first-person narrator is Scout Finch, who is five when the story begins and eight when it ends. From the first chapter, though, it's clear that Scout is remembering and narrating these events much later – after all, the second paragraph of the novel begins, "When enough years had gone by to enable us to look back on them, we sometimes discussed the events leading to [Jem's] accident" (1.2).

For the most part, Scout recounts the events from her childhood perspective, as she understood them at the time, rather than imposing an adult commentary. This makes the narrative perspective a naïve one: often we get descriptions of events just as she experiences them, without commentary on what they mean, or a commentary that is humorously innocent. But having the adult perspective be there in the background, even if it isn't in play for most of the narration, means it can pop out when it's needed to point out important things that the narrator realizes only later, to make sure that the reader sees them too.

Genre

Coming-Of-Age; Southern Gothic

To Kill a Mockingbird is first and foremost Scout's coming-of-age story. Over the course of the novel she learns to act in a more adult way, even a more ladylike way, and to see the people around her as actual human beings. Jem, too, experiences a similar process, a few steps ahead of Scout. While the novel is about the particular growing pains of Scout, Jem, and even Dill, it's also about growing up more generally. The novel asks, is it possible to become an adult, to join an adult community, and still keep a child's sensitivity to injustice? While Scout and Jem face some disappointments as they learn more about how their world works, they also develop identities that might be able to hold back the world's darker influences.

To Kill a Mockingbird also shares some characteristics with the Southern Gothic genre. It's got a haunted house and a ghost (even if both turn out not to be as frightening as first thought), it's got inexplicable evil (in the unprepossessing form of Bob Ewell), and it's got terrifying nightmare encounters (the midnight raid on the Radley Place, Bob Ewell again). It's also got ham costumes and being pantsless in public, though, so the potential horror of the novel is offset by its humor.

Tone

Naïve, Ironic

How can the tone be both naïve and ironic? Cue Scout, talking about Aunt Alexandra.

I never understood her preoccupation with heredity. Somewhere, I had received the impression that Fine Folks were people who did the best they could with the sense they had, but Aunt Alexandra was of the opinion, obliquely expressed, that the longer a family had been squatting on one patch of land the finer it was. (13.28)

Lacking a personal investment in Family Pride as her aunt thinks about it, Scout naively describes her understanding of her aunt's belief in literal terms: one could come up with flowery words about how it's about stability, a family putting down roots and becoming leaders in the community as time passes, but really it's just about a group of people getting there first and holding on to what they've got. That doesn't sound all that fine, does it? So while Scout herself is naïve in the way she narrates what's going on, the overall effect is ironic: mocking established beliefs by portraying them in an absurd way.

Writing Style

Factual

Scout's narration usually doesn't comment much on the action, just presents what happens as a series of facts. Here's an example.

Aunt Alexandra sat down in Calpurnia's chair and put her hands to her face. She sat quite still; she was so quiet I wondered if she would faint. I heard Miss Maudie breathing as if she had just climbed the steps, and in the diningroom the ladies chattered happily.

I thought Aunt Alexandra was crying, but when she took her hands away from her face, she was not. She looked weary. She spoke, and her voice was flat. (24.74)

Like Aunt Alexandra and Miss Maudie, Scout's just heard that Tom Robinson has been shot and killed. Instead of Scout talking about her own feelings at the news, there's a series of sentences describing the actions of the two older women. It's almost like we're there, watching the scene as it happens, but as ourselves rather than through the filter of Scout's interpretation. Describing the scene as if we're seeing it first-hand makes it seem more immediate, like it's happening to us, rather than to Scout. Without Scout telling us what she feels (and therefore giving us a hint as to what we should feel), we're free to come up with our own emotional reactions to the situation – and maybe even to imagine that Scout feels the same way as we do.

What's Up With the Title?

The title of *To Kill a Mockingbird* comes from something both Atticus and Miss Maudie tell Jem and Scout: "it's a sin to kill a mockingbird" (10.7, 10.9). There's more on mockingbirds as a symbol in "Symbols, Imagery, Allegory," but why make this phrase the title?

And why isn't the book called *It's a Sin To Kill a Mockingbird* ? That would make the meaning clearer, right? Or perhaps the meaning is supposed to be vague, to make the reader picking up the novel in a bookstore or library wonder what it means. Why would anyone want to kill a mockingbird? – which is, of course, a useful question to keep in mind while reading the book. So before the novel even begins, the title starts raising questions about the uses, or perhaps uselessness, of violence.

What's Up With the Epigraph?

"Lawyers, I suppose, were children once." – Charles Lamb

First off, it's from an essay by Charles Lamb, an English writer in the late-18th and early-19th century. But what does it mean? Everyone was a child once, right? So why act like it's strange that this fairly obvious fact is also true about lawyers?

Well, there is the time-honored tradition of making fun of lawyers as not quite human (even Shakespeare got in on that fun). More to the point, lawyers can seem the opposite of children: while kids are innocent and say just what they feel (no matter how embarrassing), lawyers plot and scheme and say whatever they need to in order to win their case (or so the stereotype goes). Linking lawyers to children suggests these two opposites perhaps aren't so different after all, and reminds us that lawyers really are people just like everyone else.

What's Up With the Ending?

With Ewell out of the way, all is smooth sailing for the Finches, right? Well, perhaps. While Ewell's death may end the immediate threat to their well-being, there's a whole lot of Maycomb out there that maybe thought Ewell was trash, but also thought Tom deserved to fry. Will Ewell's death cause them to reconsider their attitudes? Or will it all be business as usual in Maycomb? What happens after the end of a novel is always speculation, but based on Maycomb's behavior up to this point, it's hard to imagine that things will be much different in the immediate future.

The last line of the book, however, suggests the possibility for some kind of happy ending: "[Atticus] would be there all night, and he would be there when Jem waked up in the morning" (31.56). How hopeful is this ending? On the one hand, whatever danger may threaten, Atticus will always be there to counter it. On the other, he's basically doing damage control, watching over his unconscious son after he was nearly killed. While the ending offers a comforting image, it comes out of pain and struggle, implying that neither the comfort nor the pain wholly wins out.

Did You Know?

Trivia

- Despite repeated requests, Harper Lee has refused to write a foreword for her novel, saying that it speaks for itself. (Source)
- Harper Lee wrote the novel after her friends gave her a year's salary so she could take a break from her job and focus on her writing. (Source)
- Every year a dramatic version of the novel is performed in the old courthouse of Harper Lee's hometown, Monroeville. (Source)
- *To Kill a Mockingbird* was the first book used for a city-wide readalong, in Chicago in 2001. (Source)

- Every year there's a contest for school kids in Alabama to write an essay on *To Kill a Mockingbird* – and Harper Lee herself comes out of hiding to attend. (Source)

Steaminess Rating

PG-13

Pg-13 for mention of rape, sexual violence, and implied incest. Even though it's almost certain that Tom's rape of Mayella never actually happened, Mayella and her father describe it as if it did. Tom's testimony includes Mayella's mention of her father when she was talking about her previous sexual experience, suggesting that Ewell may have sexually assaulted her as well as beating her.

Allusions and Cultural References

Literature and Philosophy

- Bram Stoker, *Dracula* (1.32)
- Oliver Optic (1.39)
- Victor Appleton (1.39)
- Edgar Rice Burroughs (1.39)
- *Tarzan* (1.39), (4.96)
- *The Rover Boys* (1.39), (4.44)
- *Tom Swift* (1.39), (1.68), (8.104)
- Merlin (1.39)
- Seckatary Hawkins, *The Gray Ghost* (1.68), (1.87), (31.40), (31.40-47)
- *Tarzan and the Ant Men* (2.2)
- *My First Reader* (2.11)
- The Bible (2.27), (5.35), (12.126), (19.126)
- Old Testament (5.8)
- Sir Walter Scott, *Ivanhoe* (11.69), (11.80), (11.84), (11.110), (11.121)
- Shadrach (12.23)
- Garden of Gethsemane (12.54)
- Blackstone's *Commentaries* (12.132)
- Moses (12.142), (23.59)
- Arthur Conan Doyle, Sherlock Holmes (17.158)
- Mr. Jingle (18.62), a character in Charles Dickens's *The Pickwick Papers*
- Three Fingered Fred (31.49)
- Stoner's Boy (31.49-51)

Historical References

- Andrew Jackson (1.3), (28.45)
- John Wesley (1.4)
- Lorenzo Dow (2.18)
- Brigadier General Joe Wheeler (5.82)
- Bellingraths (8.44)
- General Hood (9.26)
- Stonewall Jackson (9.26)
- Lord Melbourne (9.174)
- Dixie Howell (11.34)
- Windy Seaton (11.130)
- Governor William Wyatt Bibb (13.30)
- Lydia E. Pinkham (13.32)
- Herbert Hoover (14.1)
- Henry W. Grady (15.22)
- Braxton Bragg (16.6)
- Robert E. Lee (17.58)
- Thomas Jefferson (20.50)
- John D. Rockefeller (20.51)
- Albert Einstein (20.51)
- Eleanor Roosevelt (24.55)
- Adolf Hitler (26.14-56))
- Elmer Davis (26.36)
- Bob Taylor (27.3)
- Cotton Tom Heflin (27.17)

Pop Culture

- *One Man's Family* (4.102)
- Hunt's *The Light of the World* (12.54)
- "Jubilee" (12.75)
- "On Jordan's Stormy Banks" (12.89)
- "Nearer My God to Thee" (15.45)
- "Amazing Grace" (24.25)
- "Sweetly Sings the Donkey" (26.12)
- Uncle Natchell (26.13)

Best of the Web

Movie or TV Productions

To Kill a Mockingbird, 1962
http://www.imdb.com/title/tt0056592/
This film adaptation is almost as classic as the book itself, thanks to a powerful performance by Gregory Peck as Atticus.

Videos

Opening Credit Sequence
http://www.artofthetitle.com/media/film/60s/mockingbird.html?keepThis=true&TB_iframe=true&height=430&width=730
Film buffs and adaptation enthusiasts say that *To Kill a Mockingbird*'s opening credits sequence is one of the greatest of all time. Watch it here.

"A Portrait of Harper Lee"
http://www.learnoutloud.com/Catalog/Biography/Artists/A-Portrait-of-Harper-Lee/26404
Charles J. Shields talks about his biography of Harper Lee.

Film Trailer
http://www.imdb.com/video/screenplay/vi2767651097/
A few scenes from the 1962 film adaptation.

Audios

Atticus's Closing Remarks
http://www.americanrhetoric.com/MovieSpeeches/moviespeechtokillamockingbird.html
Gregory Peck delivers Atticus's closing remarks in Tom's trial, from the 1962 film version.

Images

Harper Lee
http://upload.wikimedia.org/wikipedia/commons/7/76/Harper_Lee_Nov07.JPG
Harper Lee in 2007, receiving the Presidential Medal of Freedom.

Atticus and Tom
http://upload.wikimedia.org/wikipedia/commons/c/ce/Atticus_and_Tom_Robinson_in_court.gif
Gregory Peck as Atticus and Brock Peters as Tom in the 1962 movie version.

Mockingbird
http://upload.wikimedia.org/wikipedia/commons/5/59/Mockingbird.jpg
Take a good look so you don't accidentally kill one.

Websites

Harper Lee on Reading
http://cache.gawker.com/assets/resources/2006/06/20060627harper.jpg
One of the very few writings Lee has published since her one and only novel appeared in, of all places, Oprah's *O* magazine.

Annotations
http://www.lausd.k12.ca.us/Belmont_HS/tkm/
Explanations for references and unusual words in the text.

"Of Our Spiritual Strivings"
http://www.bartleby.com/114/1.html
Famous 1903 essay by W.E.B. DuBois on African-American experience.

Emmett Till
http://www.pbs.org/wgbh/amex/till/peopleevents/p_till.html
The murder of Emmett Till (1955) is one of several injustices that seem to have inspired events in *To Kill a Mockingbird* (published 1960). Till was a 14-year-old African-American boy brutally murdered by two white men in August 1955 for allegedly whistling at a white woman in a Mississippi grocery store. This PBS article gives some background on Till and his murder.

"Time to update schools' reading lists."
http://www.seattlepi.com/opinion/394832_nword06.html
In January 2009, high school teacher John Foley wrote an opinion piece in the *Seattle Post-Intelligencer* arguing that, now that President Obama is President-elect (at the time of Foley's publication), classic texts like *To Kill a Mockingbird* and *Adventures of Huckleberry Finn* should be dropped from the curriculum for using the "N-word." Read Foley's opinion piece here.

5513139R00078

Printed in Great Britain
by Amazon.co.uk, Ltd.,
Marston Gate.